WHY ENGLAND SLEPT

WHY ENGLAND SLEPT

JOHN F. KENNEDY

NEW YORK

WILFRED FUNK, INC.

TO MY
MOTHER AND FATHER

Acknowledgments

For their encouragement and advice in assembling much of the material upon which this book is based I would like to express my sincere appreciation to Professor Bruce Hopper and Dr. Payson Wild of Harvard University and to Mr. John Wheeler-Bennett for his very helpful suggestions.

I would also like to thank the staff members of the Widener Library of Harvard University for their helpfulness and cooperation. To the numerous writers I have mentioned in the bibliography I owe much.

The views expressed in this book are my own, and for them I accept full responsibility.

J. F. K.

1940

IMAGINE that as a young man in college you wrote a book of judgment on the behavior of a contemporary empire, its leaders and its people . . .

Imagine that twenty years later, when you are still young, you become President of the United States at a time when America faces grim possibilities of destruction and surrender . . .

Imagine, then, that you reread the book you wrote in college, and find that you would not be embarrassed by having it exposed again; this surely would be an extraordinary experience. Perhaps nothing like it ever happened before in the lives of all the leaders of men.

This has been the experience of John F. Kennedy, thirty-fifth President of the United States. And it is now an experience which every literate American can have the privilege of sharing; a special privilege, since the book is much more than merely presentable. It is today, as it was twenty years ago, good—very good.

Both President Kennedy and his fellow Americans will benefit from this experience. It will deepen the dialogue between them. The President (we can almost hear his thoughts) will be asking himself whether, in very different circumstances, he will do better than Baldwin and Chamberlain, so that a Winston Churchill will not be required to come after him and rescue a frightened nation from the jaws of death. As for the fellow American, he will find, as he reads this book, that President Kennedy has posed for *him* a searching question: will the American of the '60's behave better than the Englishman of the '30's? For Englishmen of all classes—rich and poor, intellectual and common man, Tory and left-winger—all of them contributed a full share to the failure and peril of Britain.

In writing the history of World War II, Winston Churchill opens by designating it as "The Unnecessary War." Whose the blame for so unnecessary a war? By no means England's alone. The behavior of France is even more painful to remember and, in my view, the conduct of Franklin D. Roosevelt's America prior to the blitz of 1940 was about as feeble and useless as it could possibly have been. But in this book Kennedy confines himself to a study of England; it is a scholarly study, remarkably comprehensive for its size, and remarkably judicial. He was not out to hang anybody; he was out to learn, and learn he did, and learn we still may.

Even though thoughtful men read the lessons of history differently, there is no better guarantee of the future than that men should care about the past and be able to talk to each other intelligibly about it.

As I reread *Why England Slept,* what seems to have been most especially on the student-author's mind was "democracy." Kennedy is committed to the long-range merits of democracy, but he is deeply and properly perturbed by its short-term defects. Time and again he points out the advantages which dictatorships have over democracies, and the weaknesses inherent in the democrat's individualistic or massed selfishness.

President Kennedy would, I think, agree with me that today democracy in the West is in far better shape than it was in the '30's. The '30's marked the high tide of the "revolt of the masses" in the West. The revolt was expressed in many ways—in fascism, in communism, in cynicism, in the intellectual repudiation of the great Liberal Tradition of the West, in the seeming irrelevance of Christianity, etc., etc. Today the morale of European democracies and of the United States is incomparably better than it was when President Kennedy wrote his book and when Western Democracy came near to perishing as much from its own inner betrayal as from outward aggression.

For this basic and general reason, President Kennedy is now in a better position to do what ought to be done than were the leaders of the shameful '30's. And he is better off in a number of particulars. Kennedy, the author, sees democracies as especially unwilling to arm ("there are no lobbies for armaments"), but today the one thing Americans will vote for more certainly than for anything except farm subsidies is armaments.

But whether a democracy will fight, whether, given massive arms, a democracy will use them to good effect—that is another matter. Thus, though circumstances change, Kennedy's main thesis holds true: the wise and effective leadership of a democracy is, of all human tasks, the most difficult. There is at least one cruelly exact parallel today: even when they got around to a huge rearmament effort, the people of England refused to do anything about civil defense; the same thing holds true in the United States in 1961.

On the whole, I think we can believe that the leaders and the people of the West are in a better position and in better spirit now than they were in the '30's. But our dangers are also greater. The world-wide menace of Communism is no less evil than the menace of Hitlerism, and is far more difficult to cope with. And, unlike England, we have no America as a potential savior.

When Churchill took over after the blitz, one hope sustained him besides his own resolution—the hope he placed in the United States. Even before Pearl Harbor, Churchill was able to conclude one of his great speeches by a famous quotation: "But westward, look, the land is bright." The United States has no similar hope to look to. In our hour of maximum peril, which now comes on apace, we cannot look to any points farther West for hope and help.

Of the first edition of this book, I said: "It is with genuine admiration for an important job well done that I would express to Mr. Kennedy the gratitude which everyone will feel who reads what he has so carefully and so sincerely written." Today I commend this book for its own sake, and because it will stimulate the dialogue between the people of America and their President, out of which great leadership can come.

In that anxious and anguished summer of 1940, I also said: "Not much longer shall we have time for reading the lessons of the past. An inexorable present calls us to the defense of a great future."

And now John F. Kennedy is President of the United States. In all that he does to speed the victory

of our cause, let us support him with all that we are
and have.

HENRY R. LUCE

New York, N. Y.
August 1, 1961.

Excerpts from the
Foreword
to the Original Edition

AMERICA feels herself today to be thoroughly aroused and awake. And yet, at this writing, there is every reason for serious Americans to learn a little better than they have the lesson of the painful and degrading things which can happen to those who sleep or half-sleep, and to those who in waking are still in the grip of stupefying torpors. For all Americans who are wide awake enough to read—and that, thank God, would seem to include most of us now—this book is invaluable.

I hope 1,000,000 Americans will read this book. They won't. But 100,000 citizens may well read this book. In doing so, they will have performed an act of national preparedness quite as valuable as the easy flip-flapping of another appropriation bill through Congress.

Why England Slept is a remarkable book in many respects. In the first place, it is the most dispassionate and factual account yet written of the development of British policy in the light of democratic

British public opinion in the last decade. Secondly, the book is remarkable for having been written by one so young. I cannot recall a single man of my college generation who could have written such an *adult* book on such a vitally important subject during his Senior year at college. In recent months there has been a certain amount of alarm concerning the "attitude" of the younger generation. If John Kennedy is characteristic of the younger generation—and I believe he is—many of us would be happy to have the destinies of this Republic handed over to his generation at once. This book has the rare and immensely appealing quality of combining factuality and breadth of understanding with the truest instincts of patriotism.

.   .   .   .   .   .

Not much longer shall we have time for reading the lessons of the past. An inexorable present calls us to the defense of a great future. But there is no need to turn from the past disheartened. The story of the last twenty years is not the story of *inevitable* defeat and frustration of the hopes of men. The story of the last twenty years is the story of what might have been—what truly actually really might have been, what time and again almost was. We arm ourselves, in body and spirit, not to rescue some small paltry bankruptcy settlement out of the wreckage of the past. We go forward to win in actual achievement nothing less than the brave-in-heart have hoped for and striven for before us. We shall go forward with regiments of "realists," with whole divisions of determination. And let no one doubt that our united army shall also have squadrons of dreamers who alone are equipped to mount up as eagles to look beyond the ranges: behind us and ahead—seeing behind us the long way we have come from servitude, and seeing ahead of us the promised lands of Peace and Freedom.

HENRY R. LUCE

Greenwich, Connecticut.
July 7, 1940.

Table of Contents

Foreword to the 1961 Edition   ix

Excerpts from the Foreword to the Original
Edition   xv

Introduction   xxi

PART ONE
Period of Disarmament Policy

Chapter I.   Certain Fundamental Beliefs
of the British Regarding
Armaments   3

Chapter II.   Influence of the Financial Crisis on Armaments, 1931–32   25

Chapter III.   Influence of the General Disarmament Conference and
the Pacifist Movement on
British Armaments, 1933   41

Chapter IV.   Beginnings of the Shift from
Disarmament to Rearma-
ment, 1934   59

Table of Contents

Chapter V. Influence of the General Election—Final Phase of Disarmament 87

PART TWO
Period of Rearmament Policy

PAGE

Chapter VI. The Launching of the Rearmament Program, 1936 115

Chapter VII. Slowness of Fulfillment of the Program, 1937 147

Chapter VIII. The Penalty—Munich, 1938 165

Chapter IX. The Aftermath—Britain Awakens 195

PART THREE
Conclusion

Chapter X. America's Lesson 215

Appendix 233

Bibliography 247

Introduction

WHY WAS ENGLAND so poorly prepared for the war? This question has been asked again and again in America as we watched Hitler's mechanized juggernaut churn into Holland and Belgium, break through the unbreakable Maginot Line, and on towards Paris. Always the emphasis, in the accounts of German victory, has been on the tremendous superiority of the Germans in armored equipment. Continually we heard how greatly outnumbered was the Allied Air Force. And after the retreat from Flanders, the one remark on every soldier's lips was, "If we only had had more planes." Why was there such a superiority in German armored equipment? Why didn't the Allies have more planes? What had England been doing while Hitler was building up this tremendous German Army?

About two years ago Winston Churchill published a book entitled *While England Slept*. This book is an attempt to explain *why* England slept. I have started with the assumption that there is no shortcut to the answer to this problem. To me, it appears extremely shortsighted to dismiss superficially Eng-

land's present position as the result of one man or
one group of men's blindness. To say that all the
blame must rest on the shoulders of Neville Chamberlain or of Stanley Baldwin, is to overlook the obvious. As the leaders, they are, of course, gravely and
seriously responsible. But, given the conditions of
democratic government, a free press, public elections, and a cabinet responsible to Parliament and
thus to the people, given rule by the majority, it is
unreasonable to blame the entire situation on one
man or group.

In this country, of course, great emphasis has always been placed on the individual. Personalities
have always been more interesting to us than facts.
And, in the last few years especially, events have
moved too fast to permit any detailed study of the
situation. But this story of why England did not rearm is of more than academic importance to us in
America.

The investigations of the last month in America
have shown that we are in no position to criticize
blindly. It was a great shock to America to wake up
one morning in May and find that her supposedly
invulnerable position between two large oceans was
invulnerable no longer. America's armored position
showed a startling similarity to England's after Munich. Like England, we had less than one hundred

modern planes. Like England, we had few anti-
aircraft guns. Like England, our mechanized equipment was almost nil. And yet, like England, we had
voted what we considered to be large appropriations
and we had felt perfectly secure. And, unlike Britain's leader, Stanley Baldwin, America's Roosevelt
had been far ahead of public opinion in this country
in his opposition to the dictatorship. Since his "Quarantine the aggressor" speech in 1937, he has introduced larger defense estimates than Congress was
prepared to accept. In fact, his 1940 Naval appropriation was cut by over 500 million dollars not four
months ago. I point this out as I wish to show that
we should not dismiss England's position as being
merely a question of lack of leadership. Our leadership has been outspoken, yet our positions still show
a remarkable similarity.

This is not, however, the most important reason
why a study of England's road to war is vital. I am
not an alarmist. I do not believe necessarily that if
Hitler wins the present war he will continue on his
course towards world domination. He may well be
too exhausted, or he may be satisfied with what he
has obtained. But, in the light of what has happened
in the last five years, we cannot depend on it. A defeat of the Allies may simply be one more step towards the ultimate achievement—Germany over the

world. Therefore, if Hitler succeeds in winning the present war, the position of America will be remarkably similar to that of England during the last decade.

There are, of course, great differences. There are no longer either a League of Nations or Disarmament Conferences to keep armaments down. We are far better suited industrially to match Germany's mass production methods. But, like England, we will be a democracy competing with a dictatorship. Like England, our capitalist economy will be competing with the rigid totalitarianism of the dictatorships. Like England, our armaments will have to be paid for out of our national budget. Like England, a towering national debt may appear to us more dangerous than any external menace. Like England, we have general commitments that we may not be able to fill. For example, we have warned the Japanese to stay out of the Dutch East Netherlands, yet, if they seized it, would the cry, "Are the Dutch East Indies worth a war," go up, strangely similar to the old cry in England at the time of Munich, "Are the Sudeten Germans worth a war?" And, like England, we have always considered ourselves invulnerable from invasion. But the airplane changed this position for England and may change it for us.

We have, however, one great advantage over the

English. We have the benefit of their experience. From their mistakes we should be able to learn a lesson that may prove invaluable to us in the future. From an analysis of their story we may be able to see how much of the fault is peculiarly England's and its leaders, and how much can be attributed to those principles we share in common, a democratic form of government, based on a capitalist economy.

But if we are to profit by her experience, we must take a far more tolerant attitude than we have in the past. In reading statements like that of Sir Arthur Balfour, Chairman of the Balfour Steel Company, made in 1933, "One of the gravest menaces to peace today is the totally unarmed condition of Germany," we should not dismiss it as being blindly stupid. We must remember that in the summer of 1939 a sufficient number of the Senate of the United States believed that there would not be a war in Europe this year, and refused to repeal the embargo on arms. Every country makes great errors, and there is usually a good reason for it at the time. We must also remember that we are looking at the problem from the vantage point of 1940. In reading statements like Balfour's we should try to realize that in 1933 the facts may have appeared to warrant an entirely different interpretation.

We have always had a peculiar attitude towards

England. Though on the same side of the fence with
her in opposition to Germany, our pre-war criticism
of her and her leaders was nearly as vigorous as that
which we directed towards Hitler and the Nazis. The
controversial settlement at Munich illustrates this
clearly. The word controversial does not fully express the intensity of the hate and bitterness that
have colored evaluations of the Pact in America.
This was due in great measure to the fact that Munich was regarded as a decisive event in the battle
between Democracy and Fascism. For this reason,
many of the facts and judgments underlying the
Munich settlement have been lost in a cloud of political emotionalism.

In the debate that followed the agreement, especially in America, to be pro-Munich was to be pro-
Hitler and pro-Fascism. To be anti-Munich was to
be pro-liberal and pro-Democracy. Upon few other
topics did the ordinary man, as well as the expert,
have such intense opinions. Americans simplified the
issue, compared it to a game of poker, and decided
that Chamberlain had played his cards badly and
had been outbluffed. A nation of poker players,
therefore, had little respect for the English leader
or for his policy. But they did not examine the cards
he held. This would have shown that the British

Prime Minister had little on which to gamble the existence of a great empire.

The Nazi administrator of the former Czecho-slovakian state, Baron Von Neurath, expressed the opinion that the only reason the British didn't fight at Munich was because they were unable to do so. He writes: "Those who shared in the Munich Agreement believed that an atmosphere of understanding had at long last been created and that this hopeful start would be followed by deeds. They were speedily undeceived by the turn of events. Immediately after his return to London, Mr. Chamberlain announced a huge program of rearmament. At the same time, the defects of Britain's military preparedness became plainly visible. *It was then no longer possible to conceal the true reason for her 'peaceful' attitude at Munich. She had simply been unable to embark on a European war at that time.*"

I do not agree with Von Neurath that Chamberlain's policy of appeasement at Munich was entirely the result of his military unpreparedness, but there is no doubt that that was a decisive factor. The Munich Agreement is discussed later in the book, but I mention it here to point out that America's opinion and discussion on the Agreement was an oversimplification of the case. It was this poor condition of

British armaments that made the "surrender" inevitable, which should have been the subject of the attack, rather than the Pact itself.

This book is no apologia. I do not wish to whitewash either the leaders or the public; nor do I, on the other hand, wish to oversimplify. I rather wish to trace the gradual change in the nation's psychology from the peaceful year of 1931, when the National Government came into office, to the events of the past May. Year by year, I will note the change that came about in Britain regarding armaments, analyzing the reasons for the tremendous miscalculations of the British leaders in regard to Germany. And I will try to estimate to what extent this failure to rearm was responsible for Chamberlain's policy of appeasement.

Thus, bearing in mind the strangely similar condition America may be called on to face, let us study the story of British rearmament. England made many mistakes; she is paying heavily for them now. In studying the reasons why England slept, let us try to profit by them and save ourselves her anguish.

*"I do not criticize persons,
but only a state of affairs.
It is they, however, who will
have to answer for deficiencies
at the bar of history."*

—LIDDELL HART, 1933

WHY ENGLAND SLEPT

PART ONE

Period of Disarmament Policy

I

Certain Fundamental Beliefs of the British Regarding Armaments

BEFORE BEGINNING any discussion of British rearmament, it is important to know what the psychology of the nation was at the commencement. Because of the inertia of human thought, nations, like individuals, change their ideas slowly. In a Democracy, especially, where a majority must share the idea before it becomes part of the national viewpoint, it is necessary to study the fundamentals upon which the public's opinions are based. In Germany's case, for example, the old ideas and beliefs were completely destroyed by the Treaty of Versailles and the post-war settlement. The subsequent inflation period of 1924 and the economic collapse of 1931 combined to make the German nation fertile ground for new ideas. Hitler, therefore, found it easy to convince the people that their way back to the top in Europe was through national regimentation, based upon a policy of rearmament. Rearmament answered all of Germany's problems; through it the evils of Versailles would be wiped out, through it unemployment would end, through it Germany would be able to attain her destiny. And so Germany rearmed.

But the task with England was different. Her ideas had not been shaken by the war, her system of government was the same, England's position in the world was regarded as assured. To be bothered as little as possible and to be allowed to go his peaceful way was all that the average Englishman asked. He was not haunted by the desire for a revision of treaties; he never worried about his nation's destiny. Armaments to him were not a means of national regeneration, they were an unproductive drain on a budget he was trying his hardest to balance. I stress this rather obvious difference in the viewpoints of the two nations because it is in such large measure responsible for the present condition. *For the Englishman had to be taught the need for armaments;* his natural instincts were strongly against them. Internally, armaments were a menace to his economic security, as they must be paid for out of higher taxes; externally, they were a menace to his conception of a peaceful World order based on the League of Nations.

In our study of the conversion of Britain from a disarmament psychology to one of rearmament, we will see how Hitler gradually came to be considered a greater menace than larger taxes or an unbalanced budget, and how the average Englishman began to lose faith in Britain's security based on collective guarantees.

But it takes time to change men's minds, and it takes violent shocks to change an entire nation's psychology. The experience of the United States is ample evidence of this. In spite of the events of the last few years, and in spite of the war then waging in Europe, the Congress this winter cut our Naval appropriation 500 million dollars, from $1,300,000,-000 to $800,000,000. Yet in May, due to the shock of the *Blitzkrieg*, Congress rushed through appropriations of $5,000,000,000 which were cheerfully supported by the entire nation.

Unfortunately for England, she got no sudden shock such as we did. Until Munich, there was a series of minor blows. As Hitler pointed out with some truth, in his cleverly worded letter to Daladier in August, 1939, shortly before the outbreak of the war, much of what he had done in Europe rectified wrongs that had been done at Versailles, and which should have been righted long before.

However, as Hitler pointed out, no post-war statesman had been powerful enough or sure enough of his own domestic position to make any great concession to Germany. Thus at first, many people objected to Hitler because of his method of doing things, rather than what he actually did. And this sort of indignation does not result in the state of mind that calls for huge armaments. It is only fear, violent fear, for one's own security, such as the British experienced at Munich and we have felt since the middle of May, that results in a nation-wide demand for armaments.

Before commencing, therefore, any discussion of the year-by-year conversion of Britain to a rearmament policy, there are certain fundamental opinions regarding armaments widely held by many Englishmen that must be considered. They were to have a tremendous effect on armaments in the Thirties, with the result that an understanding of them is vital to us as a background of our study.

Probably the most important of these was a firm and widely held conviction that armaments were one of the primary causes of war. The efforts of Czar Nicholas to convoke an armament conference at the end of the nineteenth century are evidence that this is not a recent theory.

The statement of Lord Grey, British Foreign Minister, made in 1914, that, "The enormous growth of armaments in Europe, the sense of insecurity, and fear caused by them; it was these that made war inevitable," had a tremendous effect on post-war British opinion. Armaments were looked upon as something horrible, as being the cause of war, not a means of defense. Again and again, through the Thirties, opponents of rearmament quoted Grey. This same theory, which had considerable truth in it, was also popular in America. In 1938, in voting against a Naval appropriations bill, Senator Borah said, "One nation putting out a program, another putting out a program to meet the program, and soon there is war." Borah and Grey may have been right, armaments may be a cause of war, but England's failure to rearm has not prevented her from becoming engaged in a war; in fact, it may cost her one. The causes of war go deeper than armaments. But there is no doubt that this view was held by a considerable portion of the British leaders and the public, and as such it is extremely important.

The second belief strongly held by many in Britain was that any increase in armaments was a blow to the League of Nations. The importance of this attitude can be seen when one recalls how strongly pro-League the British public was until 1936. A glance at the different parties' platforms for the 1935 general election bears evidence of this. The importance of the League was the central theme of all election manifestoes. And most of these League supporters felt that "without disarmament, in short, the League can have no reality." As Madariaga, Spain's great expert on disarmament, pointed out, Article VIII, calling for the reduction of armaments, is really the first clause of the Covenant, as the first seven clauses deal with the mechanics of League machinery. "A waste of money, and life, a sham and a blot on mankind, a danger for peace, armaments were the first evil which the drafters of the League Covenant sought to secure."

Thus, from the very beginning, the League's success and disarmament were seen to be synonymous. The League was supposed to be the machinery for providing collectively the security that the nations had formerly been unable, by means of armaments, to provide individually. As the nations would act collectively against aggression, their strength, it was felt, would be overwhelming. Therefore, in theory, there was no excuse for any country's rearming. To do so indicated either aggressive tendencies or a failure to believe in the League. As the English public believed strongly in the League, and as there was certainly no school which favored aggression, it was only natural that the sincere and ardent League followers would be wary of British rearmament. It is interesting to note later on that always, until the public had become disillusioned with the League after Abyssinia, the plea for armaments was put in the form of their being "necessary in order for England to carry out her League obligations."

Closely linked with this attitude towards armaments and the League, was the great hope the British people put into their efforts towards disarmament in general and the Disarmament Conference of 1932–1934 in particular. In this day of huge defense appropriations, and with our knowledge of recent events, this may seem slightly ridiculous. But this feeling was not confined to England alone. Testifying in May before a House Committee, the United States Navy's Rear-Admiral Stark said that the postwar disarmament movements were largely responsible for the poor conditions of our national defense. To understand the strength of these movements, and of the Conference, it is necessary to give a quick summary of the efforts made to achieve disarmament immediately after the war.

"The question of armaments has from the first day been the crux of the European situation, irrevocably tied up with the question of security, and round it all other international discussions have always resolved." Point IV of Wilson's Fourteen Points had called for a reduction of all armaments "to the lowest point consistent with domestic safety." "Domestic safety" is subject to different interpretations, but as these Points are the basis upon which Germany has since claimed she surrendered, it can be said that from the beginning it was felt the Allies had assumed an obligation to disarm. Then there is the Treaty of Versailles. The preamble to Article V of the Treaty says, "In order to render possible the initiation of a *general* limitation of the armaments of all nations, Germany undertakes strictly to observe the military, naval, and air clauses which follow." This clause was reinforced by another:

> The Allied and Associated Powers . . . recognize that the acceptance by Germany of the terms laid down for her own disarmament will facilitate and hasten the accomplishment of a general reduction of armaments, and they intend to open negotiations immediately with a view to the eventual adoption of a scheme of general reduction. It goes without saying that the realization of this program will depend in large part on the satisfactory carrying out by Germany of her own engagement.

The Germans have since argued that this implied an almost contractual obligation for the Allies to disarm when they had, and they point to their message of May, 1919, which said, "Germany is prepared to agree to the basic idea of the army, navy, and air regulations, provided that this is the beginning of a general reduction."

The Allies replied to this that, "The Allied and

Associated Powers wish to make it clear that their requirements in regard to German armaments were not made solely with the object of rendering it impossible to resume her policy of military aggression." These requirements, they pointed out, were only the first steps towards the reduction and limitation of armaments. By this reduction and limitation they sought to bring about one of the most fruitful preventatives of war, and to promote this reduction and limitation would be one of the League's first duties. Thus there is a definite and important question raised as to whether this implied a contractual relationship—were the Germans (as they later argued and believed) only disarming on the condition that the other nations would disarm also? If the others did not, was the contract broken, and did the Germans have the right to rearm? The question is debatable—the nationality of the debaters seeming to have as much influence on their arguments as did the facts. One writer insists "that no contractual relationship between the disarmament of the vanquished and that contemplated by the victors" existed. Another says, "A legal argument may be constructed to prove that they, the Allies, left themselves free, but there can be no doubt that on any natural reading of the Covenant the Germans and all nations had the right to expect they would disarm." This seems to me to be the correct interpretation of what was intended by the signatories.

Efforts have been made to claim that the obligation was not contractual. According to the British Statement of Policy, September 18, 1932: "To state what the object or aim of a stipulation is, is a very different thing from making the successful fulfillment of that object the conditions of the stipulation," but there seems to be little doubt that this was merely an attempt to keep the record clear. The feeling existed in Britain that if there was not a contractual obligation, there was at least a moral one for the Allies to disarm. The League recognized this also. Article VII of the Covenant states that "The member of the League recognizes the maintenance of peace requires the reduction of armaments to the lowest point consistent with national safety."

Thus Germany could point to the three great post-war documents, and in all of them the need for disarmament is mentioned. It is true that, in the Fourteen Points and in the League Covenant, the disarmament clauses are modified by the requirement of reducing only "to the lowest point consistent with national safety," yet the general feeling among the English public was that German disarmament would and should be followed by the disarmament of Britain and the rest of the world. What happened—did the Allies follow Germany's example? This is an important point, as Hitler has never overlooked an opportunity to refer to it. The simple answer is that Britain and her Allies failed completely to disarm. As I have stated, it was felt in the Twenties, due to the security supposedly guaranteed by the collective action of the League, that nations might agree to disarm. But "Fifty per cent of the power and influence of the League vanished when America withdrew." From that time on Britain's devotion to the League and willingness to take part in it were limited by several factors. One was "the one foot in the sea and one on shore" idea, which brought with it all the contradictions of alternate isolationism and the extreme policy of interference. Jules Cambon, in discussing England's policy, partly explained this when he said, "The geographical position of a nation is the chief factor determining its foreign policy, and is, indeed, the chief reason why it must have a foreign policy at all." This statement is extremely applicable to America's foreign policy as well.

Another factor governing Britain was the unwillingness of the Dominions to take part in collective guarantees. From this refusal, much of the apparent contradiction of later British policy can be understood. As late as September, 1938, the Dominions were unwilling to become involved in any struggle that appeared to them primarily European. In their denial of the Draft Treaty, the British quoted from a Canadian letter to the Secretary General of the League:

> It is intended that the obligation to render assistance shall be limited in principle to those countries situated in the same part of the globe. While Canada is situated in the North American Continent, she is a nation forming part of the British Empire, and it seems difficult to devise a scheme which would give due effect to these conflicting considerations. In any case, it seems very unlikely that the Canadian people in the present circumstances would be prepared to consent to any agreement binding Canada to give assistance, as proposed, to other nations, and the Government, therefore, does not see its way to a participation in the Treaty of Mutual Guarantee.

These factors, combined with the fear of being dragged into a war in which they had no direct interest, caused the English to feel that their "obligations" could not be extended to every frontier.

The unwillingness of Britain to take part in guarantees had a tremendous effect on France. America had guaranteed her position on the Rhine, in the Triple Guarantee after the war, but we withdrew from this when we decided on our isolationist policy. England, therefore, stated that she was no longer bound, and from that time on France felt that her *securité* lay in her own armaments. Her great fear

was Germany's superior war potential. She realized
that, because of Germany's larger population, her
greater birthrate, and her richer material resources,
she would quickly be far stronger if France and Germany
were to start on an even scale. The events of
the past seven years show how right the French were
in their estimate of Germany's potential strength.
The French felt, therefore, that if they couldn't get
strong guarantees from both England and America,
it would be suicide to disarm. And yet, all during
the Twenties, great efforts for disarmament were
made in every country. In 1926, Germany, led by
the moderates, Bruening and Stresemann, entered
the League, and her central theme was that the
Allies should grant her equality by carrying out
their disarmament promises. With the exception of
Germany, in no country was the feeling for disarmament
stronger than in Britain.

Of all the major powers in the period from 1926
to 1931, Great Britain was the only country to reduce
her armament appropriations. A glance at the
table is ample evidence of this. Germany's defense
budget is, of course, comparatively small because of
Versailles. An air force was denied her and an army
of 100,000 men was allowed only very limited equipment.

Though the amounts in this chart are given in dollars for convenience, it should be remembered, in studying these figures, that they are of dubious value as far as comparing amounts spent in the different countries in any particular year. The cost of material and wage rates are different in each country, so that the figures merely indicate whether the estimates were going up or down in different years, and are not a basis for comparison as to which country was spending the most on armaments in a particular period.

NATIONAL DEFENSE EXPENDITURES, 1926–1931
(In millions of national currency.)

Great Britain	1926–27	27–28	28–29	29–30	30–31
			(Appropriations)		
Army	43.3	43.9	41.0	41.1	40.5
Navy	57.3	58.3	57.2	55.8	51.7
Air	15.4	15.1	16.2	16.9	17.8
Tot. Pds. St.	116.0	117.3	114.5	113.9	110.0
Tot. U. S. Dollars	564.0	570.3	556.7	553.6	535.0
Exch. Rate *	486.0	486.0	486.0	486.0	486.0
Wholesale Pr. Index †	147.0	141.0	140.0	134.0	116.0

France	1926	1927	1928	1929	30–31
			(Estimates)		
Min. War.	4,296.4	8,441.0	6,254.5	6,836.2	6,278.5
Min. Mar.	1,433.0	2,221.2	2,433.4	2,882.5	2,722.7
Min. Air.	......	......	217.9	1,317.8	2,018.9
Min. Col.	269.5	431.0	478.7	719.2	539.9
Army Occ.	479.3	481.3	451.2	507.8	114.5
Tot. Francs	6,478.2	11,574.5	9,835.7	12,263.5	11,674.5
Tot. U. S. Dollars	210.5	451.4	383.5	478.2	455.3
Exch. Rate *	3.25	3.9	3.9	3.9	3.9
Wholesale Pr. Index †	703.0	617.0	126.0	124.0	105.0

* per U. S. $100.   † 1913-14 = 100.

	1926–27	27–28	28–29	29–30	30–31
Italy					
Min. War.	2,900.6	2,508.8	2,618.8	2,505.5	2,646.7
Min. Mar.	1,227.2	1,106.7	1,128.1	1,117.3	1,338.8
Min. Avi.	719.7	612.1	686.1	639.4	639.9
Min. Col.	479.8	610.4	462.3	427.3	352.7
Civ. Mob.	1.9	1.2	.8	.6	.6
Tot. Lire	5,329.4	4,839.4	4,896.3	4,690.4	4,978.9
Tot. U. S. Dollars	207.8	251.6	254.6	243.9	258.9
Exch. Rate *	3.9	5.2	5.2	5.2	5.2
Wholesale Pr. Index †	566.0	126.0	125.0	114.0	100.0

	1926–27	27–28	28–29	29–30	30–31
Japan					
Army					
Ordinary	167.5	164.1	167.6	178.8	178.6
Extraordinary	29.3	43.9	81.4	48.3	32.1
Total	196.9	218.1	249.1	227.2	210.7
Navy					
Ordinary	127.4	136.5	143.0	147.6	151.1
Extraordinary	109.8	136.9	125.1	120.0	111.7
Total	237.3	273.5	268.1	267.6	262.9
Tot. Yen	434.2	491.6	517.2	494.9	473.7
Tot. U. S. Dollars	212.0	240.9	253.4	242.5	232.1
Exch. Rate *	49.0	49.0	49.0	49.0	49.0
Wholesale Pr. Index †	174.0	169.0	171.0	161.0	131.0

	1926–27	27–28	28–29	29–30	30–31
Russia					
Mil. & Nav.	650.7	764.8	874.5	1,046.8	......
Spec. Forces	40.8	49.3	55.4	66.8	......
Escort Troop	6.5	7.6	9.1	11.5	......
Total	698.0	821.7	939.0	1,125.1	......
Spec. Acc't	6.7	9.5	12.9	not avail.	......
Tot. Rubles	704.7	831.2	951.9	1,125.1	......
Tot. U. S. Dollars	362.9	428.0	510.2	579.4	......
Exch. Rate *	51.5	51.5	51.5	51.5	......
Wholesale Pr. Index †	174.0	172.0	179.0	185.0	......

* per U. S. $100.   † 1913-14 = 100.

	1926–27	27–28	28–29	29–30	30–31
Germany					
Defense Dept.					
Ord. Exp.	617.3	645.5	757.8	683.2	710.2
Ext. Exp.	29.1	60.4	......	......	......
Total	646.5	705.9	757.8	683.2	710.2
War Charge	11.5	7.2	11.2	7.7	6.1
Tot. Reichs.	658.0	713.2	769.1	690.9	716.3
Tot. U. S. Dollars ...	156.6	169.7	182.0	164.4	170.4
Exch. Rate *	23.8	23.8	23.8	23.8	23.8
Wholesale Pr. Index †	135.0	138.0	140.0	135.0	122.0
	1926–27	27–28	28–29	29–30	30–31
United States					
Army	267.3	293.2	312.1	327.3	345.2
Navy	324.2	332.2	366.1	375.4	382.5
Total	591.5	625.4	678.3	702.8	727.7
Wholesale Pr. Index †	139.0	139.0	140.0	134.0	118.0

These figures were derived from *Foreign Policy Report on Armaments 1931.* * per U. S. $100. † 1913-14 = 100.

From this table we see that between 1926 and 1931 the British reduced their appropriations from $564,000,000 to $535,000,000; while France went from $210,000,000 to $455,000,000; Italy from $207,000,000 to $258,000,000; Japan from $237,-000,000 to $262,000,000; Russia from $362,000,000 to $579,000,000; and the United States from $591,-000,000 to $727,000,000. Thus, while the other countries' expenditures were rising, Britain's did fall slightly. This "unilateral disarmament," that is, the fact that England had been the only country to make any reductions at all, had a dual effect on Great Britain. With some people the fact that they had made their great effort in the "Twenties," was an excuse for rearming in the "Thirties." With others it had the opposite effect; it made them unwilling to change a policy in which Britain had taken the lead until it was absolutely necessary. We shall see how important this conception of "unilateral disarmament" was by the continued references later made to it.

In addition to the effect it had on British opinion, this "unilateral disarmament," small though it was, did have an effect on the actual armed efficiency. It should be noted, also, that while the British interpretation of their "unilateral disarmament" has always been one of taking "risks for peace," the opinion in other countries was that it was merely because they wished to increase their Social Services. In any case, the belief that England had led the way towards "unilateral disarmament" was widely and sincerely held by the British public and must, therefore, be considered.

The demand for disarmament became strong in nearly all countries, however, at the end of the Twenties. In response to this, a basis was finally arranged upon which, it was believed, some sort of agreement might be worked out. The Conference was called for 1932 and it was regarded not only as the culmination of a decade of effort, but as the last hope for world peace. The financial crisis accentuated this. America was demanding to know how Europe could vote huge sums for armies and yet refuse to pay her war debts. Bruening was Chancellor of Germany and he came to the Conference fully determined to attain for Germany the equality through which a balanced order might be worked out in Europe.

Hope was strong in England, too, and it had a great effect on her arms appropriations during this period from 1932 to 1934. It was felt that to increase these while the Conference was in session would be to strike a direct blow at the prospect of its success. We shall see the strength of this idea when we come to look at yearly estimates.

There are two other important factors that must be considered briefly in a study of British opinion of this period. The first is the extent of the pacifist movement in Britain which was stronger there after the war than in any other country. The grip it had on the public in general and the Labour Party in particular must continually be borne in mind. The second is the British consciousness of separation from the continent. Previous to this period the protection of her navy had enabled Britain to take a detached view of events in Europe. Centuries of this type of isolation had resulted in what Sir Arthur Salter calls the "psychology of island immunity." The effect of this was that Britain felt she could delay with her armaments longer than any other country. She was invulnerable from invasion. Americans have had this same feeling of immunity, and both countries, as a result, have considered their navies first, often at the expense of the other services. If the navy was strong, the country was safe.

The belief that the navy was her primary unit of defense was, of course, much stronger in England than here, due to her centuries of sea-faring history. Even as late as 1936 and 1937, priority was given to naval orders over those of the air. An attitude bred into peoples' bones and a part of their national tradition dies hard. In England's case it did not vanish completely until the fear engendered by Hitler's air power wiped it out during the Munich crisis. As long as this attitude remained, it had a great effect on national psychology. The people failed to recognize the necessity of making sacrifices to provide armaments in general and an air force in particular.

This is a brief explanation of some of the factors which must be borne in mind in studying British rearmament. They are some of the ideas held by a great portion of the British public and its leaders. They are more or less inbred and must be changed before the nation is embarked on an active unified program of rearmament. And until this national feeling of unity can be attained, a democracy is hopelessly outclassed in trying to compete with a dictatorship. In one country, the effort is divided and disorganized, in the other it is united, even though it is accomplished by propaganda and force.

To recapitulate, the ideas most widely held were: first, the idea that armaments were a cause of war; second, the belief that rearmament was a blow to the League; third, that Europe must achieve disarmament in the Conference that was called in 1932 if she was ever to have peace; fourth, the feeling that Britain had undertaken unilateral disarmament in the Twenties and should try to continue that policy; fifth, the great strength of the pacifist movement; and sixth, the feeling of separation from the continent and consequent immunity.

No discussion of Britain's psychology would be complete unless some mention were made of the natural feeling of confidence, even of superiority, that every Englishman feels and to which many Americans object. This feeling, while it is an invaluable asset in bearing up under disaster, has had a great effect on the need Britain felt for rearming. The idea that Britain loses every battle except the last has proved correct so many times in the past that the average Englishman is unwilling to make great personal sacrifices until the danger is overwhelmingly apparent. This notion that God will make a special effort to look after England, and that she will muddle through, took a great toll of the British re-armament efforts of the Thirties.

1 9 3 1

Mar. 21	Austro-German Customs Union Plan (Sept. 3—abandoned)
July 20	French Memorandum on Disarmament; Seven Power London Conference
Aug. 21	National Government formed under Ramsay MacDonald
Sept. 19	Invasion of Manchuria by Japanese
Sept. 21	Britain abandons Gold Standard

1 9 3 2

Feb. 2	Disarmament Conference
Mar. 13–	
April 10	Hindenburg reelected
July 3	German Elections (Nazis won 230 seats)
July 9	Reparation Agreement signed at Lausanne
Nov. 7	General Von Schleicher succeeds Herr Von Papen as Chancellor
Nov. 8	Election of Franklin D. Roosevelt as President of the United States

For the convenience of the reader, a calendar containing the most important events of the year has been placed at the beginning of certain chapters.

Though not every event is discussed, the calendar will aid in establishing the tempo of the time.

II

Influence of the Financial Crisis on Armaments, 1931–1932

THE NATIONAL GOVERNMENT, which was to be responsible for England's policy during the period we are studying, came into power in the general election of November, 1931. It replaced a Labour Government and gained the tremendous Parliamentary majority of 554 seats to 56 for the opposition. These figures, however, do not tell the true story of the relative strength of the parties. Actually, the votes were only 14,127,586 to 6,698,457. The *raison d'être* of the new National Government was the failure of the Labour Government to reach a satisfactory solution of the grave economic problem that England was facing along with the rest of the world.

The platform upon which the National Government took office was that of rigid economy and a balanced budget. Germany, under Hitler in 1932, chose to meet the economic crisis by a vigorous program of rearmament; America, under Roosevelt, chose the method of pump-priming by expenditures on public works. These solutions were adjusted to the economic problems with which those countries were faced. Likewise England's plan of a balanced budget and strict economy was peculiarly adapted to England's financial position.

England in world trade fills a position somewhat analogous to the middle man in private industry. She is not a naturally rich country like America or even Germany. She is obliged to import most of her vital raw materials. For example, two-thirds of her total food supply must be imported, which means nearly 50,000 tons of food a day. These imports must, of course, be paid for. She has two sources of capital; the first and most important is the return on her numerous and large investments abroad. The second is from the receipts from her export trade, which she has tried unsuccessfully to have equal her import trade. If this trade fell off, England's economic position would become hopeless. For this reason she was willing to go to extraordinary lengths to keep this trade up. But it meant that in order to compete with the rich countries, like the United States, or the cheap-labor countries, like Japan, she was obliged to keep her manufacturing costs down to the lowest possible point. Therefore, England was obliged to avoid any measures that meant a rise in prices or that might carry danger of inflation.

For these and for other related reasons, therefore, England chose the method of strict economy for her road back. She introduced the dole, in contrast to our W.P.A., and the whole tempo of her spending was built around this idea of a balanced budget. I have discussed at some length this desire for economy as it was to have a great effect on British armaments in subsequent years. It took a great shock to force Britain to change this fiscal policy, especially for such an unproductive expenditure as armaments.

As I stated, the National Government came in in November 1931. What was the general disposition of the country regarding armaments when they took office? An examination of the estimates for the service—which correspond to our appropriations—submitted the previous March, is revealing. From these we can judge the general temper of Parliament in particular and the country in general.

The estimates for the year 1931–1932 were £109,-635,000 as compared to £110,297,000 for 1930, a net decrease of £66,200, and the attitude of the Labour Government was one of apology that they had not carried the reduction further. For example, in Commons in March, 1931, Mr. A. V. Alexander, the First Lord of the Admiralty and the present First Lord of the Admiralty under Churchill, said that while no doubt many would be disappointed that the net saving in the estimates over last year's figure was not more than £342,000, he blamed it on the former Conservative Government for drastically curtailing ordinary expenditures. Likewise, in regard to the slight increase in the air expenditures of £250,000, Mr. E. Montague, Under-Secretary for Air, stated that the increase was really economical considering the additions to be made in the strength of the air force, and he expressed a hope that the coming Disarmament Conference would do much to remove the serious disparity between the Royal Air Force and foreign air services. The figures on the relative strength of the different countries' air arms were at this time:

France	2,375
United States	1,752
Japan	1,639
Italy	1,507
Great Britain	1,434 *

Thus it can be seen that the estimates for the services were on about the same general scale as in previous years, and that the sentiment was one of regret that greater reduction could not be made.

Probably the strongest force in keeping down the

* Germany was, of course, denied any air force by Versailles, and thus Great Britain is in fifth position. This was not a cause of much real concern, due to her friendly relations with France and the United States.

armament estimates was the desire for economy due to the financial panic, and this was to be the great factor in the coming year of 1932.

This drive for economy was aided and abetted in the convoking of the Disarmament Conference in March, 1932—which gave new impetus to the Disarmament policy. The first estimates that the National Government submitted were for £104,364,-300, as compared to £109,635,000 for 1931–1932, a net decrease of £5,270,700 over the previous year. In explaining the decrease of £1,128,700 in the navy estimates, the First Lord of the Admiralty, Sir Bolton Eyres-Monsell, said:

I now come to the most dismal part of my speech, and that is the figure of the 1932 program . . . it is my misfortune to introduce the Lowest Estimates that have been introduced since 1913, and which have obviously been framed, not on what we would like but with a view to contributing very generously towards the nation's common effort to meet the great financial crisis. . . . *The drop . . . is due to the imperative need for economies.* Since the war we have built only seventeen cruisers.

This speech indicates the reason why the government was willing to reduce the fleet almost to the danger point. They felt that the risk of financial disaster was far greater than the menace from any rival power. The comments of the Opposition throw even more light on the subject, as it appears to be more or less an accepted rule that the Opposition, because it has no responsibility, will vote so that its record will be clear and will appeal to the country. In this case, Mr. G. Hall, former Civil Lord to the Admiralty in the Labour Government, said the reduction fell far short of what was expected. Mr. Shaw, the former Minister of War, and others bore him out. The army estimates were a somewhat similar story—being £36,448,000 as compared to £39,930,000, but the Secretary of War in his Memorandum warned that the reductions were made at a drastic suspension or retardation of many services essential to the army, that they were made for reasons of economy, and were not to be taken as a standard.

The Air estimates told a similar story. They showed a net figure of £17,400,000, a decline of £700,000, which was made possible only by the postponement of many services which, under normal circumstances, would be regarded as essential. A new reason for the reduction of armaments, in addition to the desire for economy, was given in the Secretary's Memorandum accompanying the estimates. In it he said:

His Majesty's Government having subscribed to the Armaments Truce, no new units are being formed in 1932. In the normal course, a minimum of two new Home Defense squadrons would have been added under the program initiated in 1923, but subsequently three times retarded, with the result that ten regular squadrons still remain to be formed for its completion.

The 1923 program referred to was a defense scheme set up by Lord Asquith, which called for the establishment of fifty-two squadrons for Britain as a minimum requirement. This program for 624 planes was to be staggered over a period of years. This is important as Britain's air defense program was based until late in 1934 on this antiquated defense scheme.

He then went on to mention the disparity between England and the rest of the world in air strength and finished by saying:

His Majesty's Government would view the situation with anxiety but for their earnest hope and expectation that the Disarmament Conference now in session at Geneva will bring about a reduction in air armaments.

The Under-Secretary of Air, Sir Philip Sassoon, warned that the estimate would have to go up in 1933, and stated that the defense scheme was ten squadrons short of the 1923 minimum program, and that England's air expenditures had gone down while others had gone up two and one-half times, and that "we were taking great risks."

It thus can be seen that, in the year 1932, the defense forces were greatly reduced for two reasons:

first, the need for economy; and second, the Disarmament Conference in which it was hoped there would be an internationalizing of air forces and a reduction of armaments generally that would make any increase unnecessary. We find, however, that as the Conference progressed through the spring of 1932, the earlier hopes for any great immediate success began to appear over-optimistic.

The Conference was bothered by the same trouble that had plagued the efforts to achieve disarmament in the Twenties. No one wished to renounce the weapons upon which they were most dependent. England felt her navy had been cut to the bone by the Washington Conference of 1922 and the London Naval Conference of 1931. France would not give up her army unless the other countries gave her more definite guarantees. Russia embarrassed everyone by demanding complete disarmament. This was a very radical step for a disarmament conference, but it was tempered by the obvious fact that Russia's chief weapon was propaganda, which did not depend on armed force.

The great trouble, of course, was the inability of the delegates to agree on fundamentals, such as what constituted an offensive weapon. As one delegate pointed out, it all depends on which end of a revolver one is facing whether it is an offensive or a defensive weapon. Because of the inability of the different countries to come to an agreement, Chancellor Bruening was unable to satisfy the vigorous demands for equality of the home front in Germany. He was forced out of office in May, 1932, and was succeeded by Von Papen, who paved the way for Hitler in 1933. Thus, the Disarmament Conference witnessed one prelude to the European drama that was shortly to unroll.

Another indication of what was to come was the Japanese invasion of Manchuria in September, 1931. This, at first, seemed to be a localized affair; it is only after having watched the Ethiopian invasion, the invasion of the Rhineland, and all the other events leading up to the present war, that we can see this was the beginning of the end. This invasion was to deal a blow to the League from which it never recovered. It was to show that the basis on which England and the other powers had built their security was worthless, and this was bound to have a tremendous effect on the defensive position of Great Britain.

It is not proposed here to go into a discussion of Britain's foreign policy as regards Manchuria. Her failure to take the lead in stopping Japan when America, through Stimson, extended the promise of co-operation has been regarded as one of the great blunders of post-war British diplomacy. Sir John Si-

mon turned down Stimson's offer of co-operation
and America retired into her traditional isolationism. England's reasons for doing so were varied. The
English people naturally desired to avoid going to
war, and the British Foreign Office did not know
whether the American people would back Stimson
to the end if it meant a war with Japan.

British industry disliked cracking down on a good
customer, and most people in Britain failed to see
that this was the great test for collective security.
Then, too, many English leaders, with their fear of
Russia and the spread of Communism, desired to see
Russia with a militant Japan on her border. Others
felt that China was "backward" and in a state of dis-
order, and with England's history she would be hypo-
critical to deny Japan's expansion. These factors
combined to result in a "do nothing" policy.

This policy has been beaten from pillar to post for
a variety of reasons, not the least of which was Sir
John Simon's extremely unfortunate and undiplo-
matic presentation of the British Government's case.
I refer to his speech on the subject of the Arms Embargo to Japan and China in the Commons in which
he said: "However we handle this matter, I do not
intend my own country to get into trouble about it,"
and also his speech on the Lytton report, after which
the Japanese delegate, Mr. Matswoka, stated that Sir

John Simon had expressed in one half-hour what he had been trying to tell the League Assembly for weeks.

However, the reason that the slow rise to power of the National Socialists and the invasion of Manchuria are important to us, is the effect they had on the Armament expenditures. I have discussed these events in some detail, not because they were widely regarded at that time in England as being grounds for rearmament, but because it is the fruit from these two seeds that grows to vital importance in the subsequent years.

Before the end of 1932, the first real questions concerning the condition of British armaments emerges. The progress, or rather the lack of progress, of the Disarmament Conference began to worry some Britishers, even before the end of the year. The Lausanne Agreement in June, which settled some of the most pressing monetary problems between England and Germany, had only slightly eased disappointment over the work of the Conference. In November, Captain Guest, an air expert, expressed doubt in Parliament about the condition of Britain's air armaments, and said that the program was twenty per cent below safety. It is interesting to note, however, that Captain Guest made little reference to Germany; he used France as the measuring rod.

Baldwin, the next day, made a speech in reply that had a tremendous influence on later British policy:

> I think it is well for the man in the street to realize that there is no power on earth which can protect him from being bombed. Whatever people may tell him, *the bomber will always get through.* . . . *The only defense is in offense,* which means that you have to kill more women and children more quickly than the enemy if you want to save yourselves.

This speech, with its note of hopelessness, was quoted again and again through the succeeding years by various parties and organizations who were voting against rearmament. The idea that "the bomber will always get through" "deeply . . . and profoundly impressed the House," and more deeply and profoundly impressed the people. It struck them with a feeling of horror towards war and especially was this directed against the air arm. It also did much to strengthen the pacifist movement in the country. It was shortly after this speech that the Oxford Union, a political club at Oxford, passed their now-famous resolution that "this House will not die for King or Country." The importance of this must not be exaggerated as the skill of the debaters is ordinarily the subject of the vote, and much of it is in a facetious vein. But that such a startling resolution should come from an English audience indicates the strong pacifist sentiment throughout the country at this time.

The feeling of hopelessness felt by many people in regard to air raids can be traced from this speech right through the dark days of the crisis in September, 1938, when the fear of air raids played such an important part in forcing the Munich settlement. We can trace it further in the actual equipping of the R.A.F., with the emphasis placed on the bombers, the offensive arm, rather than on fighters, the defensive arm. This, too, was due to the idea that "the bomber will always get through." The result was that Britain's defense position was greatly weakened. At the time of Munich she had only one fighter for every two of her bombers. It was not until the beginning of 1939 that this situation was remedied and the ratio of fighters to bombers raised to three to five.

Baldwin's speech was answered by Winston Churchill in what was really the opening gun of his campaign of demanding rearmament, although he makes no direct mention of it here. His references to Germany were merely fear for the future, not the warning of actual warlike preparations, which was featured in his later speeches. He does, however, repeat his idea that he "would very much regret to see any approximations in military strength between

Germany and France." He is carrying through the old French fear of Germany's war potential that had characterized the French attitude toward disarmament during the Twenties.

We must not get the idea, though, that this was a period of fear over the condition of Britain's armaments. The emphasis in the government was still definitely strong for effecting disarmament, though it was with more hope than confidence that they approached it. Their attitude was that they would do their utmost to effect disarmament, but meanwhile they "would not continue their policy of unilateral disarmament." There had been, of course, nothing to cause any great change in their feelings. They were marking time while waiting for the report of the Lytton Commission which was investigating the Sino-Japanese disagreement over Manchuria.

As for Germany, Hitler had not yet assumed office. Any stiffening in the government's attitude toward unilateral disarmament, as displayed in Baldwin's November 10 speech, was merely a reflection of some disappointment in the progress of the Disarmament Conference. Yet hope had been by no means abandoned, as was to be shown the next year. Churchill and Guest have been quoted merely to show that here we first begin to get the separation into the three groups: the extremists of the right, led by

Churchill, who favored a strong armament policy; the moderate or Government group; and the Opposition, which, while it did not favor complete unilateral disarmament, was led by an out-and-out pacifist, George Lansbury.

1933

Jan. 30   Hitler becomes German Chancellor

Feb. 24   League Assembly Resolution on Manchuria

Feb. 27   Burning of German Reichstag; suppression of Communist Party

Mar. 17   Japan gives notice of withdrawal from the League

June 12   Opening of World Economic Conference in London

Oct. 14   Germany withdraws from the League of Nations and Disarmament Conference

Nov. 16   United States recognizes U.S.S.R.

III

Influence of the General Disarmament Conference and the Pacifist Movement on British Armaments, 1933

THE YEAR 1933 was a fateful one. On the thirtieth of January Adolf Hitler became the Chancellor of the German Reich and from the Far East, Japan gave her notice of withdrawal from the League. The tragedy had begun in earnest. And yet the Defense estimates submitted for the year 1933–1934 showed no rapid rise. There was an increase of around five million pounds to about 99,000,000 pounds, but in all the memoranda and speeches accompanying the estimates there is the same attitude of apologetic explanation for the rise in the estimates that we have noted in the previous years.

In explaining the increase of three million pounds for the Navy, the First Lord of the Admiralty pointed out that it was made necessary due to the fact "that a large part of the normal expenditure upon shipbuilding in 1932 was deeply retarded and heaped on into subsequent years by the temporary

expedient of deferring the orders of the 1931 program." There was considerable politics in this statement, as it placed the blame on the shoulders of the
Labour Government which had been in office in 1931,
but nevertheless its apologetic tone indicates the
strong antipathy of Parliament and the country for
anything that appeared like rearming. In an impas-
sioned speech in Commons, Sir Bolton-Eyres-Mon-
sell, the First Lord, in pointing out further postponement of naval construction, as in 1931–1932, stated:

The people who always deny us the right to an adequate
national defense are precisely the same people who inter-
nationally are always clamoring for sanctions, for block-
ades, for wars to end war. They always profess to be wor-
shipping the Goddess of Peace, but to my mind, their real
deity is an ancient heathen god of Wrath and Vengeance.
But if these bloodthirsty pacifists, I might call them, ever
get their way, which God forbid, let the country realize
what part the British Navy would be called upon to play
in any form of castigation they wished to inflict, and the
First Lord of the Admiralty of the Day, standing at this
Box, would not be asking for an increase of 3,000,000
pounds but for a sum of money that would well-nigh break
the heart of the British taxpayer.

This speech seems to me to indicate much of the
struggle then going on in England. The country itself was strongly pacifistic and pro-League, basing its
idea of security on collective guarantees. But the
Navy group, as can be seen from the bitter tone of

Monsell's castigation of the pacifists whom he felt were wrecking the Navy, was becoming anxious as it realized the relatively poor position that the Navy would soon be in if the cuts in the appropriations continued.

In the memorandum and speeches on the Army appropriation, we see the same tone of apology for the increase of £1,500,000 over that of the previous year. In his memorandum, the Minister of War, Viscount Halisham, stated, "Owing to the fact that some of the reductions made last year were of a temporary and transitory character, to meet the special circumstances of the financial crisis, they have risen by £1,462,000 although they are still less by nearly £2,000,000 than the Estimates for 1931." In a speech in Commons, March 9, Mr. Duff-Cooper, the present Minister of Information under Churchill and the then Financial Secretary of the War Office, gave a clear picture of the general attitude towards armaments. He said that he did not suppose any member of the opposition would criticize the government for introducing the estimates when they remembered that in 1931, when a Socialist Government had been in office for two years, and when the international horizon *was certainly no more clouded than it was today*," they introduced estimates which were defended by the Socialist War

Minister, Mr. Tom Shaw, on the ground that they had been cut down to the lowest possible point, which were £2,000,000 greater than those introduced today. *The increase in expenditure did not represent any augmentation whatever* in the establishment of the British Army in the scale of munitions or in preparations for war. It was simply made to replace the cuts made last year "in the face of the danger of national bankruptcy which was then *rightly thought to be an even greater danger than having an inefficient fighting service.*" This speech, as the italics indicate, shows first, that the international situation, even with the advent to power of Hitler, was not considered in Britain any darker than in 1931; and secondly, how important the financial factor was in keeping down armament appropriations.

The Air estimates carried through the general pattern of the other two services. The estimates for 1933–1934, which totalled £17,426,000, showed an increase of £26,000 over those for 1932–1933. However, the Secretary of Air endeavored to explain away even this slight increase by stating in his memorandum:

The apparent increase of £26,000 in the net total actually conceals a reduction of nearly £340,000, since expenditure hitherto borne on the Vote for Colonial and Middle

Eastern Services has this year been transferred to Air Votes.
. . . This further substantial reduction in air expenditures
can only be justified in the *light of the continuing need for
exceptional measures of economy,* and the postponement
of a number of important services has been unavoidable.
. . . As in 1932 every precaution has been taken to ensure
that the economies shall not react adversely on safety or
unduly impair efficiency. . . .

The memorandum also stated that the Air Defense scheme of Lord Asquith, calling for a certain
number of plane squadrons to be built yearly, would
be held in suspense for another year, *"a decision
which was a further earnest of the whole-hearted desire of the United Kingdom Government to promote disarmament and to bring about a reduction in
the world's air forces on an equitable basis."* In the
meantime, he warned, the Royal Air Force remained
at a figure of strength less than that of other great
nations, despite the rapidly growing importance of
air power to the British Empire with its far-flung
responsibilities.

In the Commons, March 14, Sir Philip Sassoon,
Under-Secretary of Air, said that the need for economy, which had left so clear a mark upon the estimates which he introduced last year, was no less
pressing today, and had had a similar influence on
the present estimates. In summing up the estimates,
it may be said that, in general, they carry through

the same tendencies that were behind the 1931–1932 estimates. The need for economy, which was the primary concern of the National Government, and the hope for a successful conclusion of the Disarmament Conference, combined with the general pacifist feeling among the people to make any great increase in the estimates impossible.

However, as the year progressed, there were some rebellions against this feeling. Warnings were uttered concerning the serious relative condition of the defense services. But most of the articles were written by "strong navy" or "strong army" men who would be for increases no matter what the international situation. For example, in discussing the condition that the Navy was in, a writer in *The Saturday Review,* a vigorous weekly publication, called attention to the figures of Sir Phipps Hornsby, who had claimed England's estimated cruiser need was 186. He stated that due to the Conferences of Washington and London, they were now accepting a limit of 50. The importance to us of this type of article lies in the fact that only very occasionally was Germany referred to as a menace; the above-mentioned writer used France and Japan as his yardstick. He also mentioned the strangely diminished trust in the Naval Defense. Chiefly responsible for this, he felt, "were the Pacifist doctrines, which were then so strong for the great reductions."

The Army also came in for its share of criticism, but again it was more from experts, men like Liddell-Hart. Liddell-Hart was an extremely important figure in the pre-war picture. He was very close to the War Office and his plans for army reform were largely carried through when Hoare-Belisha became Minister for War. His book, *The Defense of Britain,* best expresses his views. Liddell-Hart held that for a country situated as was Britain, with a strong navy, her greatest strength would lie in building up her defenses in order to prevent a knockout blow, and then blockading the enemy into surrender. This theory was excellent, but it has become clear that merely to prevent a knockout blow, Britain's war efforts must be far greater than Hart ever estimated. Hart was the great advocate of the limited warfare theory, which would call for a very small interference with the normal life of the country. He, therefore, believed in small mobile units, highly mechanized.

His great importance to us lies in the fact that while his efforts at army reform were vigorous and far-sighted, yet his basic theory of limited warfare gave many English people the feeling that arma-

ments were something that were of no great concern
to the average citizen, as his life would not be inter-
fered with, whether he was at war or peace.

In 1933, Liddell-Hart wrote a searching article on
The Grave Deficiencies of the Army, which informs
us of what the condition of the British Army was at
that period. That condition, evidently, was not very
good, as he labeled the five existing divisions "suicide clubs." He pointed out that the number of guns
to a division was not sufficient for a barrage of one
Infantry battalion and that there were twelve battalions to a division. Liddell-Hart does not blame
the economy drive as much as the "inertia not of the
individuals, but of the system."

The British Army at that time was regulated by
the Cardwell system. This provided that regiments
should be split up between home and foreign service, with the men to be interchanged and alter-
nated. Although this had the obvious advantage of
giving all of the men in each regiment wide experience, it also meant that it took a long time for reforms to be effected. It is worth contrasting in this
respect the position of the German Army when
Hitler came into power. During the years of the
Weimar Republic, under the Versailles Treaty, Germany was permitted an army of only 100,000 men.
This number included 10,000 officers, and as each

soldier was obliged to enlist for twelve years, these officers had comparatively little to do as far as training troops was concerned. During these years, therefore, while the French officers were busy training over 200,000 conscripts a year, and the British officers were busy patrolling the Empire, the German officers had little to do but to evolve new theories of warfare. Ordinarily, military leaders are extremely reluctant to accept innovations. They continue with their old accepted techniques and methods, and this was true of the general staffs of France and England. Especially in the latter country, where tradition governs everything, the old methods of doing things frequently presented an immovable obstacle in the path of reform. The German General Staff, on the other hand, was not hampered by this as it had realized that any hope of its attaining success lay in its adoption of the newest methods of warfare. So from the beginning, mechanized warfare was seized on by the Germans; to the English the idea had to be "sold" and that could be done only gradually.

A type of technical analysis similar to Liddell-Hart's was directed toward the problem of developing an air-consciousness among the British public. In an article, *England in the Air,* Lord Halsbury hit on an important point. He called attention to the low number of Class A pilots in the country, compared to the growing number in Germany, and explained that much of the lack of air-mindedness in England was due to the geographical and atmospheric conditions, which were unfavorable as compared to Germany. Another important article brought out the fact that while America spent one-half as much on subsidies for her air mail service as on her air force, England was completely neglecting to build up this branch as a nucleus for a reserve Air Force. While the writer fails to point out the difference in size between England and America, which makes this comparison inapplicable, this and the article by Lord Halsbury do point out some of the important differences in the problem of developing an air force and pilots in England as compared with Germany and America and should be considered in analyzing future relative progress.

As far as can be judged, most of the articles in the important reviews of this period were written either by the "big navy" type of writers who are always booming for an increase; or were written by military technicians of the type of Liddell-Hart who were keen on reforming the army, not so much because they felt there was any immediate, pressing need for rearmament, but rather because they felt that in its present condition, the inefficiency of the system prevented the taxpayer from getting his money's worth.

Then, too, there was another reason, as stated by I. Phayre in *Armaments and British Foreign Policy.* "Britain's status of a 'has been' darting daily to Geneva to report new decay in her armed might, has had disastrous reactions—even in our vital export trade." The effect of these articles on the public in general seems to have been slight, although they had more effect on certain groups in the Conservative Party. For, as the year wore on, a change was beginning to be felt.

The government's attitude had been one of considerable optimism at the beginning of the year. This was reflected in the estimates we have seen, which were submitted in March. But the failure of the MacDonald Disarmament Plan, submitted to the Disarmament Conference in March, and the Japanese notice of resignation from the League on March 27, 1933, introduced a note of gloom into the previously bright horizon. Churchill continued to make speeches. He felt that the government was being extremely inconsistent in its attitude towards France. On the one hand, it was urging France to disarm, while, on the other, it was refusing to give France the guarantees she demanded before she felt she could afford to disarm. While he agreed they should extend no guarantees, he felt it was only logical that they should stop demanding that France disarm. There were also indications that the change for the worse in foreign affairs was beginning to cause some worry in Conservative Party circles. This can be seen from the Resolution passed at the Sixtieth Annual Conference of the National Union of Conservatives and Unionist Associations: "That this Conference desires to record its grave anxiety in regard to the inadequacy of the provisions made for Imperial defense."

I do not mean to give the impression that the country had reached a point where it felt rearmament was necessary. Even Churchill's warnings were not the vigorous demand that they were to be later. The whole spirit of the country was pacifistic—probably more strongly than it had ever been. Numerous books against war like *Cry Havoc!* by Beverly Nichols, were widely circulated and avidly read. In an article on *Illusions of Pacifists,* the writer began, "Disarmament and peace are among the most discussed topics of the day."

In addition to the pacifist group publications, *The Economist,* which is the great authority on business opinion in England, continually wrote articles pointing to the necessity for the success of the Disarmament Conference. It was not that the people were ignorant of the possible menaces of Hitlerism; it was rather that their reactions to that menace took a different form from demanding armaments. As an example, on October 16, immediately after the German withdrawal from the Conference, George Lansbury, Leader of the Opposition, expressed himself strongly against Germany:

We who belong to the peace movement cannot for a moment consent to the rearmament of Germany.

On October 18, he went on to say:

On behalf of the British Labour Party, I say we shall oppose the rearmament of Germany. We demand that the British Government shall take the lead and call upon all its associates themselves to disarm and thus carry out the pledges given to Germany in 1919. This is a matter of honour. . . .

But he then continued:

We will not support an increase in armaments but we shall also refuse to support our own or any other Government in an endeavour to apply penalties or sanctions against Germany. No one will ask for these if the great nations immediately, substantially disarm and continue until universal disarmament is accomplished.

Thus, while it was realized that Germany had committed a breach in withdrawing from the Conference, it was merely an opportunity for the Socialist to condemn the policy of the Conservative Party. This is further borne out by Sir Stafford Cripps' remark on October 14, "that Germany's withdrawal from the League was largely laid to the charge of this country, and certainly a great degree also to the charge of France. We entered into solemn obligations that if Germany would disarm we and other countries would do the same, but year after year went by and nothing was done."

The executive committee of the National Liberal Federation on October 18 adopted a resolution which deplored Germany's withdrawal but repudiated the suggestion that this disaster marked the failure of the League; they rather blamed the "governments, including England's, who had failed to make adequate use of the machinery for national co-operation." The point is that while all groups condemned Germany's withdrawal and some thought it "had destroyed for the moment the moral influence of the League," no one, except a few of the extreme "right," considered it grounds for rearmament.

The cleverness of Hitler's propaganda was extraordinary, and it played on the natural sympathy that many in England felt at first for Germany's efforts to recoup her fortunes. Many people in England felt that Nazism was only a vigorous nationalist movement which would shortly burn itself out. Others thought that it was largely a Fascist movement carried on under the direction of Germany's leading capitalists. Hermann Rauschning in his book, *The Revolution of Nihilism,* points out that there were many different groups in Germany itself who were completely duped by Hitler during the first years. It is understandable, therefore, that many in England likewise failed at first to recognize the true nature of the Revolution. Indeed, during this period, the fear of Communism, not of Nazism, was the great British bogey. Germany, under Hitler, with its early program of vigorous opposition to Communism, was looked on as a bulwark against the spread of the doctrine through Europe. Sir Arthur Balfour, in speaking of the Russian danger, said, "One of the greatest menaces to peace today is the totally unarmed condition of Germany." Today that is strangely ironic.

Thus, in summing up the year, it may be said that while the nation as a whole condemned Hitlerism, with its treatment of the Jews, its militarism, and regimentation of the national life, and while each of the different political parties condemned Germany's withdrawal from the Disarmament Conference, nevertheless, among nearly all groups the dominating desire was still directed towards achieving disarmament. With some it was for economic reasons; with others, because of the hope that they placed in the Disarmament Conference. But in the country as a whole, it was due to the fact that England, in the year of 1933, was pacifist as it never was before and probably never will be again.

The strength of this movement is shown in the returns from that year's local elections, especially the famous East Fulham election, which in 1936 was to be used by Baldwin as proof of the country's strong pacifist sentiment. Here, in a traditionally Conservative district, a Labour candidate won an overwhelming victory on a platform of "peace and disarmament." The strength of this platform may be seen by the editorial in the conservative *London Times* the next day, which stated that the Labour candidate should not have been allowed to be the only candidate to run on a disarmament ticket. It went on to say, referring to the National Government, "No government is less likely to indulge in provocative armaments or to despair of international efforts to secure general disarmament." Carrying this sentiment still further, Baldwin, in a public letter to a Conservative Party candidate, wrote: "The whole country, irrespective of party, is solidly united in favor of peace and disarmament by international agreement," and denied "as a calculated and mischievous lie any statements which said the Conservative Party did not believe in these principles."

The East Fulham election indicates the strength

of the pacifist movement and what influence it could have on elections and on party policy. I do not cite the editorial in *The Times* and the Baldwin letter to prove that the Conservative Party or Mr. Baldwin necessarily really believed in "peace and disarmament by international agreement." But the editorial shows that the strength of the pacifist movement was well-recognized in responsible quarters. And the very fact that Baldwin was obliged to write such a letter in order to make sure of this election indicates beyond any doubt that the British nation in 1933 was completely and overwhelmingly pacifist, and that this was an accepted fact by the leaders of the Parties.

We stated before that men's ideas change slowly and that a nation's ideas change even more slowly. It takes shocks—hard shocks—to change a nation's psychology. Let us turn to 1934 and see whether the leaders or external forces would give England the necessary jolts to move her from this Utopian pacifism. Up until now her attitude toward armaments has been a perfectly natural result of the forces then dominant in British life. No other program could be expected. But time is slipping by, the crucial years are coming: England must begin to awaken.

1 9 3 4

Jan. 21   Devaluation of American Dollar

Mar. 1   Pu Yi enthroned by Japanese as Emperor of Manchuria

June 14   Meeting of Hitler and Mussolini at Venice

July 19   Baldwin submits Defense Plan

June 30   "The Thirtieth of June" Executions in Germany

July 25   Austrian Putsch; murder of Chancellor Dollfuss; Dollfuss succeeded by Von Schuschnigg

Sept. 18   The U.S.S.R. admitted to the League of Nations

Dec. 4   Fighting at Wal Wal between Italians and Abyssinian troops

Dec. 14   Italy rejects Abyssinian request for Arbitration

IV

Beginnings of the Shift from Disarmament to Rearmament, 1934

THE YEAR 1934 opened quietly enough. Japan had given notice of her withdrawal from the League, but at Geneva the Disarmament Conference was continuing in session. That the Conference was still regarded as having a considerable chance for success is evidenced by the strong support given it by Anthony Eden, the Lord Privy Seal. Eden has always been considered a vigorous proponent of rearmament, so when he said it would only be *after* the Conference had been proved a failure that "every country, no doubt, will then have to proceed to review its armaments," it becomes clear how hard the idea of attaining general European disarmament was dying. In addition, the British Government on January 31 had submitted comprehensive proposals to the Conference for a solution. Therefore, although Germany under Hitler had withdrawn in October, 1933, in a highly dramatic fashion, yet the March estimates show little change in tenor from those of the previous years.

The combined net estimates showed an increase of only about £5,000,000 over those of the previous year. The estimates are of particular interest as they show that Britain was now becoming vaguely conscious of the unsettled condition of world affairs. The memorandum and speeches on the Navy estimates, which were up about £1,500,000, indicate that Britain's first instinct was to check on the condition of her Navy, her traditional first line of defense. In a statement to the Commons on March 12, 1934, Sir Bolton Eyres-Monsell, the First Lord, reassured the House by stating that, by 1936, "in all categories we shall have the full tonnage that we are allowed by the Treaty." He then went on to say:

It is true that the Navy estimates in the last two years have risen by a little over £6,000,000, but, honestly, I do not believe, looking round at the general state of the world today, that anybody who had my job, who had the tremendous responsibility of answering for the efficiency of the British Navy to the British people, could possibly ask for a penny less.

This speech does not strike the apologetic note of the previous year, although it is not at all belligerent. It indicates that by 1936 the Navy would be up to full tonnage *allowed by the Treaty*—and it is this

Treaty limitation which we must bear in mind in considering Navy estimates and building plans. It must be remembered also that, as Sir Roger Keyes, Admiral of the Fleet, pointed out in the Parliamentary Debates of July 30, 1934, the Fleet had had seven lean years, and, although they were building up to treaty limits in tonnage, much of it was over-age and ready for scrapping.

In general, however, there was still the usual confident feeling that the Fleet had no rival that might be considered dangerous. The United States was the only power who equalled her, and there was no thought of war with her. It was not until after the scare given to the British Navy by the threat of Italian submarines and of Italian air power in the Mediterranean that Britain was to become really concerned about her Fleet.

It is in the Air estimates, though, that we find the important statements. The traditional feelings of the Englishman towards the various services has already been discussed. To the average Britisher the Air was a branch of which he had a vague and indefinite fear, more from a feeling of the hopelessness of a successful defense than anything else. Bearing in mind the background of this feeling, let us look at the estimate debates, which reveal the beginning of the rearmament struggle between the different groups.

The memorandum submitted with the estimates is extraordinarily revealing of the general feeling of the British regarding the Air force. Britain was, at that time, sixth in Air strength—Russia having passed her since 1931. However, to balance that, there was no Air power within striking distance that could be called hostile. In other words due to the distance factor, Japan, the United States, or Russia could be disregarded, as none of their planes could possibly menace England directly. And Germany was forbidden an Air arm by the Treaty of Versailles. These facts should be remembered in reading the Air estimtaes for 1934–1935, which showed a net total of £17,561,000, an increase of only £135,000 over the figures for 1933–1934. In his memorandum, the Secretary for Air pointed out:

That the rise is so small, despite provision for the formation of the new units detailed below, is *due to the continuance of the most stringent economy throughout all Votes,* and to the further postponement of all services, the completion of which is not a matter of urgent necessity. . . . *Pending consideration by the Permanent Disarmament Commission of yet more far-reaching measures,* His Majesty's government have made their primary object the attainment of Air parity in first-line strength between the principal powers, in order that a race may at all costs be avoided. It is their earnest desire to achieve this end, if possible, by means of a reduction to the British level . . . of the strength of these foreign Air forces which at present so outnumber our own. Mean-

time, however, considerable programs of Air expansion have
been approved in a number of foreign countries and are already in several cases in process of actual execution. Air
expenditure abroad is in fact showing a general upward
trend on a scale which in most cases far exceeds the small
increase in the present estimates.

He then went on to say:

*Pending the results of the Disarmament Conference, how-
ever, the number of new units to be formed in this country
is being curtailed to a minimum,* and will in fact be too little to bridge the widening gap between the present strength
of the Royal Air Force and of the Air services of the other
Great Powers. His Majesty's Government have by their suc-
cessive postponements of the modest Home Defense Scheme
of 1923 . . . given proof of their sincerity of their purpose to
achieve Air disarmament . . . they are under the necessity of
making it equally plain that they cannot in the interests of
our national and imperial security accept a position of continuing inferiority in the air.

The Marquess of Londonderry, the Secretary for
Air, in a speech in the House of Lords, warned, however, that "if parity cannot be secured by reductions
elsewhere . . . then we shall have no option but beginning to build upwards." Similarly, in Commons
on March 8, Sir Philip Sassoon noted England's unilateral disarmament and pointed to the recent au-
thorization of the United States of £3,000,000 and
of the Russian and Japanese expansion. He warned
that if the other countries "will not come down

to our level we shall build up to theirs." He then went on to say, "These estimates, therefore, in broad outline, are the outcome *of our desire to pursue disarmament and to study economy on the one hand; and on the other, of our reluctant conviction that the policy of postponement of the 1923 program cannot be continued.*" He mentioned the fact that:

We have recently submitted to the principal European Air Powers a Disarmament Memorandum which would have the effect of stabilizing leading Air forces of the world ... which would entail considerable reductions in all the leading Air forces, including our own. We stand by that memorandum. ... We do not want to put forward a program of construction which might prove to be the starting gun for a race in Air armaments. In the interests of world peace, the initial measure of advance which is indicated in these estimates is designedly placed within the most modest bounds.

What inference can be drawn from the tone and content of the estimates, the memorandum, and the above speech? In the first place, we still find the need for economy referred to as one of the basic reasons for keeping the estimates down. Coupled with this, is the mention of the Disarmament Conference in general, and the memorandum of January 31 in particular, as two factors which are preventing an increase. As long as there was hope for the Disarmament Conference and as long as they were taking

part in it, the government did not want to take any
chance of being accused of sabotaging it. But there
is also a note of warning that if this latest proposal
did not bear fruit, England would have the right to
work to achieve parity.

Churchill, in his attacks on the British attitude of
complacency, received strong support from extreme
Imperial groups. Magazines like *The Saturday Review,* which was strongly Fascist and was in later
years to call for a war on Russia, cheer Mussolini on
against Ethiopia, and beseech Edward VIII to become dictator, supported him. They agreed that
"We have never been, certainly not for hundreds of
years, so defenseless as we are now."

On the other hand, we have the more moderate
publications, like *The Economist,* warning of the impossibility of rivalling the leading European Powers
in Air strength, and at the same time matching leading oceanic powers in Naval armaments. As *The
Economist* is the great financial magazine of England, its opinions may be said to be typical of the
views of business and finance. From its frequent edi-
torials against rearmament we can see that the
"City," which corresponds to America's Wall Street
but which is much closer to the Government, was
fully and completely against rearmament.

In another important article, *The Economist* criticized Churchill's "characteristic intervention (which need not be taken too tragically), for he is now accepted even abroad as our brilliant but erratic *enfant terrible. Once again he has displayed an unerring instinct for hitting on the worst possible policies."* This is very important in looking back at this period. In the light of the present-day war, we are amazed at the blindness of British leaders, and the country as a whole, that they could fail to see the correctness of Churchill's arguments. But here was a contemporary and widely held opinion on his policy.

In studying Churchill's warnings, which have proved to be so accurate, it is necessary to realize the somewhat peculiar position he has always occupied in British politics. No one has ever questioned his ability or his dynamic energy. But these very qualities, which now cause Britain to consider him the only man who can carry through a successful war policy, have in times of peace caused him to be considered "dangerous," and a little uncomfortable to have around. Then, too, Churchill has always represented the extreme viewpoint. He has never stood on middle ground—he went "all out" for anything he advocated, with the result that his opinions have always been taken advisedly by most British leaders.

During this year, for the first time, Germany's air force was considered as a potential menace. The first portion of the year's debates was taken up chiefly with the progress of the British Disarmament Proposals of January, 1934. Sir John Simon, the Foreign Minister, said on February 6, in the Commons, discussing the negotiations:

Approaching the whole thing in a spirit of realism we reach ... the inevitable deduction from two propositions, neither of which can be effectively challenged. *The first proposition is that Germany's claim to equality of rights in the matter of armaments cannot be resisted, and ought not to be resisted.*

Though this statement sounds extraordinary to us at the present time, it is a very valuable indication of the way many in England felt about Germany. The reasons for this go back to the feeling that the Allies had failed after the war to keep their promises to Germany regarding disarmament. Consequently, when it began to appear improbable that all of the Powers would reduce to Germany's level, the only equitable solution seemed to be that they should allow Germany to attain the position of equality by rearming up to their level. During this period there was much sympathy for Germany in England. In the years of 1934 and 1935 the feeling reached its height. Hitler was able to "cash in" on the good will that had been aroused by the sincere and earnest efforts of Germany to rebuild herself in the 'twenties under the Weimar Republic.

Many English leaders realized that they had failed to give Bruening the support he deserved; they did not wish to make the same mistake again. All of these reasons, therefore, and the natural rightist feeling of a good many of the British aristocracy, combined to make entirely dissimilar groups friendly to Germany. One group was friendly because of its trade connections with Germany; another because it hated Communism; another because it felt that England had treated Germany badly in the days of the Republic. For various reasons, Germany did not appear, to these and other groups, to be a cause for rearmament. Many of them felt, in fact, that to rearm would be an unfriendly act and would alienate any hope of living at peace with Germany in the future. There is no doubt that they were mistaken— that this was not the old Germany. Nevertheless, their views had a tremendous influence at the time. Therefore, they cannot be dismissed simply on the score of being shortsighted.

As the year progressed, anxiety at last began to be felt about Britain's air strength. Baldwin, himself, was conscious of this, for he promised the Commons in May that "if all efforts to get air reduction fail," he would see to it "that in air strength and air power this country shall no longer be in a position inferior to any country within striking distance of our shores." But he also brought out the reason why nothing was being done then to build up air strength. He pointed out that the Foreign Secretary "was going to Geneva in a fortnight's time for the Disarmament Conference." If this failed, he said, they would go ahead quickly. "I am also certain," Baldwin pointed out, "as I have been so before, that there is no new danger in the near future before this country. There may be less danger in the future than we imagine, and the preparations we are taking are in more than ample time."

The Commons debates in July indicate the feelings of the different groups clearer than any others. Hope had finally vanished in regard to bringing about a successful conclusion of the Disarmament Conference. Therefore, on July 19, 1934, Baldwin introduced the first of a long series of defense programs, caused by the menace of Nazi Germany. It was small compared to that of subsequent years, but it marks the beginnings of the change from a disarmament psychology to one of rearmament. Up until now the forces for disarmament were strong. The potential danger from Germany finally counteracted these forces, and the pendulum began to swing the other way. From this time on, the picture begins to change. England was stirring in her sleep.

Baldwin's speech accompanying the scheme is worth studying, as it indicates what the government's new attitude was to be. Was the new defense scheme to be strong or weak? Would it satisfy men like Churchill? Would publications like *The Economist* support it? Let us see first what it called for. In introducing it, Baldwin discussed the fact that the other nations had failed to follow England's example of unilateral disarmament. He pointed out that large deficiencies had grown up, owing to *"financial stringency* and the *discussions on armaments."* The position as far as the R.A.F. goes was a case for further development "which has time and again been postponed." He pointed out that many of the factors which compelled the present increase might change, and so the program would be kept constantly under review. He than announced a "four-year program calling for an increase of forty-one squadrons (492 planes) in addition to those already announced." [1] Thirty-three squadrons (396 planes) would be for Home Defense, raising the existing forty-two squadrons (504 planes) to a total of seventy-five squadrons

[1] English squadrons vary from 9 to 12 planes, depending on the type. I have taken 12—the usual figure—as my standard.

(900 planes). The rate of the increase, he said, would depend on various considerations, including finance.

In analyzing this speech, it must be remembered that this program was based on the 1934 idea of numbers of planes, not those of today. Where we talk in units of thousands, they are talking in terms of hundreds. The leading air forces at that time totalled around two thousand planes.

A debate on Baldwin's new defense program was held on July 30. The opposition group—that is the Labour Party—moved a resolution that gives a clear view of the policy they were going to adopt in subsequent years:

That, while reaffirming its adherence to the system of collective security under the League of Nations and accepting its obligation thereunder, the House regrets that despite negotiations for a Disarmament Conference, for European pacts of non-aggression and mutual assistance, His Majesty's Government stand upon a policy of rearmament neither necessitated by any new commitment nor calculated to add to the security of the Nation, but which will serve to jeopardize the prospects of international disarmament and to encourage a revival of dangerous and wasteful competition in preparation for war.

Briefly, what this meant was that the Labour Party was opposed to the program for several of the reasons discussed in the first chapter.

Attlee, then Parliamentary leader of the Labour

Party and the present Lord Privy Seal under Churchill, explained their stand. He first attacked the National Government for being responsible for the failure of the Disarmament Conference. He then attacked the idea of unilateral *rearmament,* which he said described the present program. He harked back to Baldwin's 1932 statement that the bomber would always get through, as an argument on the futility of rearming. His chief argument, however, which was extraordinarily difficult to refute, was that if the League was worth anything—and he assumed it was as the government still said its policy was based on it—there was no need for this rearmament, as the League's collective strength would be enough to protect the country.

This, of course, was extremely clever politically. With an election year coming in 1935, the government could not come out and say that the League was a failure, even if they had really thought so, as the country was still overwhelmingly pro-League and had tremendous confidence in it. It had to be proved a failure over Ethiopia before the British public would have accepted its desertion. Of course, there is no doubt that Labour's stand represented a sincere belief on their part that a rearmament program would be a blow at the League. This is shown by the fact that they stuck by their guns in opposing re-

armament, even when it became popular throughout the country at a later period. Nevertheless, at the
time, they proceeded politically to make the most of
their opportunity, as they had the Conservative Party
in a very difficult position.

The United States has witnessed a similar situation.
The Labour Party in England used the argument
that an increase in armaments meant that Britain
must be deserting the League on which her foreign
policy was based. Likewise, in America in 1938,
when Roosevelt put forward a heavy defense budget,
Senate leaders like Borah and Johnson, and House
leaders like Hamilton Fish, argued that this must
mean a desertion of America's traditional foreign
policy of neutrality and isolation. Again and again
in speeches, they stated that unless the President had
made new commitments, there was no necessity for
increasing military expenditures. As the President
had been very outspoken against the dictatorships in
his "Quarantine the agressors" speech at Chicago
in October of the previous year, their words sounded
logical to many.

These men, like the leaders of the Labour Party in
England, were perfectly sincere. They really believed
an increase in armaments indicated a change in the
foreign policy which might lead to war. Their opposition to the increase in appropriations was not

necessarily opposition to armaments as such. Rather, they believed that a vote against an increase in armaments was a vote against a change in America's foreign policy. And thus, like the Labour Party in England, they opposed rearming.

Baldwin, in defending the new scheme, repeated much of his speech of July 19th. He first tried to explain why such a program was necessary. He compared England's small increase of only 42 planes in the last four years to France's increase of 300 to 400, and said the new figures would raise England's figure from 844 to 1,304. He was careful not to risk offending the League advocates and made a bid for their support when he said, "Without this increase which we are proposing we shall certainly not be capable of effective co-operation in any system of collective security under the League of Nations."

Baldwin then discussed the opposition to the scheme, which he labelled as being of three kinds. There were those who said it was too much—this was the attitude of the Liberal and Labour Parties. There were those who said it was enough, but that the timing was bad, because of the effect it would have on the attempts to achieve disarmament. And then there was the Churchill group who stated, out and out, that it was not enough. Baldwin denied the latter assumption, because in the "judgement of our experts and the Government as a whole, it did provide for our future defensive needs in the *light of all indications at present available.*" He concluded in words that have become famous. They are doubly important as they indicate that Baldwin was aware of the change that Air power was bringing about in European balance. It indicates that he believed that there would have to be a change in their traditional policy of isolation from the continent. That he was not completely blind to this potentiality makes his subsequent failure to awaken Britain all the more serious. Here is what he said: "Let us never forget this, since the day of the air, the old frontiers are gone. When you think of the defense of England you no longer think of the chalk cliffs of Dover. You think of the Rhine—that is where our frontier lies."

Sir Herbert Samuel answered this speech on behalf of the Liberal Party. This is England's third political party, and, being much smaller than the other two, it had no great political influence. But it has produced some great leaders—Lloyd George is a Liberal—and it represents that important section of English opinion which cannot agree with Labour's radicalism, but nevertheless finds the strict party control of the Conservative Party and the Tory outlook of many of its leaders too narrow.

Regarding the increase in armaments, Sir Herbert Samuel put forth objections similar to the Labour Party's. He answered the Government's claim that they needed the increase in order to fulfill their collective obligations by saying, "We are not universal policemen to carry out all the obligations of the League." He asked the reason for the increase and said that neither Russia nor Japan was within striking distance of the shore. France was an ally and therefore only Germany was left. And here he brought up the question of the Treaty of Versailles. By the Treaty, Germany was not allowed to have an air fleet; if, therefore, she was building one, England would either be obliged to declare the Treaty was at an end or be prepared to go in and stop her. No one at that time in England could conceive of declaring war then and there on Germany, especially as any air activity at that time was listed under the head of "civil aviation." For this reason, Germany was not officially mentioned by Baldwin as being the object of the rearmament.

After Sir Herbert Samuel had finished expressing the viewpoint of those opposing the new program, Winston Churchill, as a representative of that small wing of the Conservative Party which felt the program insufficient, rose to speak. While they were now the sixth Air power, he warned them, this program would mean an increase of only fifty planes by 1935–1936. He also pointed out that, even if they put through the program, *relatively* in four years England would be worse off.

This is an important point. Both in England and in America, the tendency has always been to examine programs and estimates on the basis of the previous year or years. If we build five hundred planes or four battleships in one year, we tend to think that eight hundred planes or six battleships is a big increase for the next year. We think of the program in relation to its predecessor. In the present year we think of our defense expenditure as a tremendous appropriation. It is, when we measure it by the 1939 appropriation of around $1,200,000,000. But we should think of the size of the appropriation only in relation to the war efforts of other countries, not our own. In other words, one of England's great mistakes lay in measuring all yearly increases in her program and appropriation by the standards of the previous years. She, therefore, found the expansion substantial, and believed that she had made a great effort to meet the problem. She had a feeling of satisfaction and complacency that was unwarranted. She did *not* measure her efforts by the war effort Germany, in the same year, was putting out. In a democracy, where Congress or Parliament's attitude is necessarily so much a reflection of the public's general feeling, this point may be vital. In England's case, it was.

Churchill continued his attack by warning the "pacifist-minded government" that, by the end of 1935, Germany would be equal to England, by 1936 it would be stronger. He compared the difference in the size of the two in civil aviation and in the numbers of pilots, and, in conclusion, bitterly attacked Labour's motion for a vote of censure.

Another speaker supporting this view was an old army man, Brigadier-General Critchley, who called on the Government to build 1,000 planes instead of 440. He said that in 1936 Germany would be stronger and they could never overtake them—an ominous prophecy.

Sir John Simon, the Foreign Minister, replied to these speeches in a summation on behalf of the Government. He admitted that "Germany's interest in the Air development is very marked and the sums proposed to be spent upon it under the proclaimed head of 'Civil Aviation' and 'Passive Air Defense' are very striking." He then went on to attack, on one hand, the Socialist opposition who were against any increase in arms, but wanted England to take her part in collective security; and, on the other hand, the group led by Churchill whose motto he said was,

"And damned be him that first cries, Hold, enough."
He added that this was the last observation Macbeth
had made before losing his head. He concluded by
saying, "that we have framed our proposals after full
consideration of information and estimates from
all available quarters, and the purpose of our proposals is to secure, among other things, that at no
moment during our stewardship will we fail to have
a military force adequate to the circumstances with
which we might have to deal."

In November of this year, a further debate was
held and in this Churchill said that Germany had
"an illegal air force rapidly approaching equality
with our own." In the Government's reply for the
first time it was admitted that Germany had already
formed a military air force. Baldwin, however, denied Churchill's statement about approaching equality: "It is not the case that Germany is approaching
equality with us. Her real strength is not fifty per
cent of our strength today," and as for a year from
then, ". . . so far from the Germany military air force
being at least as strong as, and probably stronger
than our own, we estimate that we shall still have in
Europe alone a margin of nearly fifty per cent. I
cannot look farther forward than the next two years."

That Baldwin represented general British opinion
of Germany's strength is evidenced by an editorial in

The Economist. It attacked Churchill's statement that if the present programs continued the German military Air Force would be fifty per cent greater than England's in 1936 and by 1937 almost double. It stated that Germany was not approaching equality, that there were no grounds for panic and that "there was no immediate menace confronting us or anyone else." Likewise, an article in another popular periodical, *The Fortnightly Review,* carried through the same theme. The writer, in an article, "Does Germany Mean War?" analyzed the situation and answered strongly in the negative. Baldwin, therefore, was not alone in his figures or in his general psychology regarding Germany. But it was for his continual efforts to discount any feeling of worry that he must bear his share of the responsibility.

In 1934, there was no direct cause for alarm, England was still ahead of Germany. But there was a potential menace, and Baldwin, who had indicated his consciousness of it by his "frontier on the Rhine" speech, should have been pointing out the possible dangers to the country. Instead, he proceeded to soothe the worry that was beginning to crop up in the minds of the better-informed by stating:

The total number of service air craft which any country possesses is an entirely different thing from the total number of air craft of first-line strength. The total number, of course, includes the first-line strength and all the reserve machines used in practice and many things of that kind. I would like the House to remember that one may get a wholly erroneous picture in making comparisons, just to mention the air craft of our own country, when perhaps the figures that have been mentioned are but the figures of first-line strength.

He then went on to give the figures of German aircraft strength as being between 600 and the French government's outside figure of 1,110. The accuracy of these figures was to be attacked later in Churchill's March 19, 1935, speech as being wrong. But it is well to remember that it was on this basis and on these figures that the government was to draw up next year's estimates and programs.

This year, 1934, witnessed the end of the disarmament drive in England; from this time on the question was to be merely how much they should rearm. That disarmament was officially dead is indicated by the fact that a resolution presented at the Conservative Party's Congress in October, 1934, calling for the government "to pursue its efforts to secure the reduction and limitation of armaments by international agreements," was withdrawn. Instead, the Congress passed the resolution expressing "anxiety in regard to the inadequacy of the provisions made for Imperial Defense."

Towards this rearmament policy, the different

groups lined up as follows: On the side for extensive rearmament was a small group led by Churchill in Parliament, and in the publication field by extremist magazines like *The Saturday Review*. Then there is the National Government's official policy, which is a middle course, calling for some rearmament, but only "in order to carry out its collective obligations." On the side against rearmament there is *The Economist*, representing a certain portion of business opinion who wished to balance the budget, and who, therefore, wanted more disarmament measures, if possible. Then there are the Labour and Liberal Parties, who declared that they were against rearmament as it did not fit in with their concepts of collective security and the League. And on the extreme side we have the complete pacifists like George Lansbury, Dick Shepherd, and Aldous Huxley, who were against *all* armaments.

In summing up 1934 we can see, in the light of what was to come, that it was a fateful year. It marked the end of any hope the British government had of achieving disarmament. The part they played in bringing about the death of this hope was considerable, as they failed completely to take the lead at the Conference in the manner that had been expected. The Conference was doomed when France and England failed in the spring of 1932 to make sufficient concessions to Bruening to enable him to satisfy the German people. Nevertheless, the Conference continued and efforts were made up through 1934 to bring about some equitable solution. The Conference, therefore, did have a great effect on armaments through the years 1932, 1933, and 1934.

In addition, the other great contributing factor in keeping the estimates down, the financial crisis, had also eased. Britain had succeeded in weathering the storm, and so the unbalanced budget was not to be the great menace it had been in the past.

The situation in regard to Germany had become somewhat changed. She was for the first time talked about as a potential menace. It was, therefore, only natural that this should be the year for commencing Britain's rearmament drive.

Any armament program normally takes from three to four years to develop. A 16-inch-gun battery takes three years to build—a battleship four. Britain was later to get into difficulties trying to jam an armament program into a shorter period of time.

For the tragedy was that England *did not start her armament* drive in this the crucial year. Rather, she postponed it until 1936, and it is this two-year delay that proved fatal at the time of Munich and explains much of the reason for her present difficulty.

No one man or group can be held responsible for

the condition of British armaments. Baldwin's error lay in not pointing out the potential dangers of the situation. But the blame for the delay of 1935 must be put largely on the British public. For 1935 was the year of the General Election, and this election resulted in a postponement of Britain's armament efforts.

1935

Jan. 1	Germany conscripts labor
Jan. 7	Franco-Italian Agreement
Mar. 4	Issuance of British "Statement Relating to Defense"
Mar. 9	Announcement of creation of German Air Force
Mar. 16	Reintroduction of Conscription in Germany
Mar. 25	Visit of Sir John Simon and Anthony Eden to Berlin (Eden goes on to Moscow, Warsaw, Prague)
Apr. 11-14	Three-Power Conference at Stresa
Apr. 17	Special Session of League Council condemns unilateral denunciation
May 2	Franco-Soviet Pact signed
June 7	Reconstruction of National Government by Baldwin
June 18	Anglo-German Naval Agreement
Oct. 2	Italy invades Abyssinia
Nov. 14	General election returns National Government by 431 to 184
Dec. 8-9	Hoare-Laval Agreement in Paris
Dec. 9-20	Five-Power Naval Conference in London
Dec. 19	Sir Samuel Hoare resigns and is succeeded by Eden

V

Influence of the General Election
Final Phase of Disarmament

THE YEAR 1935, which was to witness Germany's emergence as a first-class military power, opened rather quietly; in fact, there was a considerable easing of international tension. Russia had entered the League in 1934; the Saar plebiscite had gone smoothly; France and Italy had reconciled their differences by the agreement of January 8, and, on the whole, there seemed to be considerable basis for a hope of working out some solution to the new problem of the air menace that was changing the balance of power so rapidly.

By the Pact of Locarno, in 1925, Germany, France, Britain, Italy and Belgium had guaranteed "jointly and severally" the western frontier territorial limits set down by Versailles and guaranteed the demilitarization of the Rhineland. This agreement had given France something of the security she had been striving for. Now, however, the rise of air power in a militant country like Germany presented a new threat, and both France and England wished to strengthen their positions by a new guarantee. Therefore, on February 3, an Anglo-French Memorandum was issued calling for a Western Air Pact of Mutual Assistance. Hitler, after some delay, agreed, and it was arranged for Sir John Simon to go to Berlin to discuss the plan with the Führer. Several days before he was scheduled to leave, however, the British Government issued the White Paper on Defense that Baldwin had previously promised. There is no doubt that the time for its issuance was very badly chosen. Though it had been promised the year before, it gave the Germans an excuse of which they were shortly to take full advantage.

As a matter of fact, the British White Paper was far from being a belligerent doctrine. With an "It's hurting us more than it's hurting you" tone, the government presented it to "a far from enthusiastic House of Commons." The Paper began with a long explanation of the fact that England's example in disarming unilaterally had not been followed by the other countries. For this reason the government felt it necessary to "put our own armaments on a footing to safeguard us against potential dangers." They said they intended merely to recondition the Navy and the Army and that in "the Royal Air Force alone was an appreciable increase of units deemed immediately necessary." In regard to the postponement in maintaining minimum air strength the Paper said:

It is not that British Governments have neglected to keep themselves informed of the position . . . but risks have been accepted deliberately in the aim of permanent peace. *Again and again, rather than run any risk of jeopardizing some promising movement in this direction by increasing expenditure on armaments, Governments have postponed the adoption of measures that were required when considered from the point of view of national defense alone.*

This reiterates the statements made in previous years. The White Paper then hit on a rather novel explanation for rearming. It said that:

In this way, we have taken risks for peace, but, as intimated by the Secretary of State for Foreign Affairs in the debate on the Address on November 28, 1934, disarming ourselves in advance, by ourselves, by way of an example—has not increased our negotiating power in the disarmament discussions at Geneva.

The Paper referred to the frequent aspersions that had been cast at Britain's efforts to achieve a reduction in air strength at the Disarmament Conference. It was felt at Geneva that much of the explanation for Britain's position lay in the fact that she herself was then in sixth position in Air strength. It was asserted that Britain considered it more economical to have others reduce down to her size than to build up to theirs.

The Paper called attention to the "unilateral and uncontrolled" rearmament of Germany, and the "general feeling of insecurity" caused by it throughout Europe. The Paper sought to enlist the support of the pacifically-minded public by saying in conclusion, that, while peace was the principal aim of British foreign policy, "notwithstanding their confidence in the ultimate triumph of peaceful methods in the present troubled state of the world, they realized that armaments could not be dispensed with. They are required to preserve peace, to maintain security, and to deter aggression."

The estimates which accompanied this proposal showed an increase of about £10,000,000 over the 1934–1935 figures. They rose from £113,711,000 to £124,250,000. It was only in the Air estimates, however, that there was any considerable degree of action. The Navy increase was due "chiefly to the need for repair and modernization of the capital ships, due to the prolongation of their lives by the London Treaty of 1931"; that of the Army was bringing "our military preparations more up to date."

Therefore, it was only in Air estimates that provision was made for an actual increase in size. They rose £3,000,000, from around £17,500,000 to £20,-500,000. The proposals that accompanied them in regard to the increase in the number of planes are interesting when compared to the German figures that were shortly to be announced. The estimates provided for the addition of a total of forty-one and a half squadrons (498 planes), by the end of 1938, at which time the strength of the R.A.F. would be 1330 air craft. Four squadrons (48 planes) were formed in 1934, and twenty-five more (300 planes) would be formed in 1935–1936—the program being arranged so that it would "be possible to retard or accelerate it in accordance with the requirements of the international situation." Eleven new squadrons (132 planes) would be added to the Home Defense, which would comprise fifty-nine squadrons (708 planes), making a total strength, including the Fleet Air Armament of 106½ squadrons (1278 planes), 93½ regular squadrons (1122 planes), and 13½ new regular squadrons (162 planes) of Home Defense.

It should be noted as an indication of the general attitude, that, in all the memoranda accompanying the estimates, the tone was one of explanation for the need of rearming, rather than explanations for failing to rearm sooner. This is in contrast to White Papers of later years, and indicative of how strong the feeling against armaments among the people still was.

It should be remembered that this was an election year, the General Election was to be held that coming summer. What representatives of the three parties said to these armament proposals is significant, therefore, as it gives an indication of the country's attitude. For election year is the time when the public rules—it is then that the politicians acknowledge its superiority. Then, as at no other time, do they try to strike on the policy most acceptable to the mass of the voters.

The debates, of course, were colored by the fact that Goering had announced on March 9 the existence of a German Air Force. That the Paper should receive so much opposition under these conditions demonstrates that the word "rearmament" was still unacceptable to the country, in spite of the changing situation on the continent.

Attlee, in his attack on the Paper in behalf of the Labour Party, warned against construing anything that he might say as "palliating in any way Germany's action in leaving the League, Germany's rearming, or the preaching of war in Germany." But he said that National Defense should not be sought in unilateral rearmament but rather through the

League system "in which the whole world would be ranked against an aggressor."

The position of Labour in regard to rearmament has been subject to much criticism by the Conservatives, as it was felt by them that Labour's position was paradoxical. On the one hand, the Conservatives argued, Labour was demanding that Britain carry out her collective obligations; on the other, it was voting against any measures that would bring her defense forces up to sufficient strength to carry through these obligations. In fact, so much capital was made out of the apparent contradiction in Labour's position, that Major Attlee found himself obliged to write a letter to *The Times* in May, explaining it. He repeated some of his old arguments, but he presented a very effective case. He began on the assumption that the Locarno Treaty and the League's pledge were still considered the basis for the Government's foreign policy. This is what the Government had always claimed. If the Government was behind these pledges and if they were respected, the Government did not need armed parity, as all members of the League would be against the aggressor and the force would be overwhelming. This position was, on the face of it, perfectly logical and it hit on the weak spot in the Government's case.

It would have been political suicide for the Government to have hinted at this time that it did not have complete confidence in the League. And yet, if the League really functioned, England's present armaments were sufficient, as all the other members would, in theory, have come to her aid. Therefore, no matter what its secret doubts, the Government was obliged to say that it was only because England wanted to "pull her weight" in carrying out her share of the obligations that armaments were needed.

Opposition to the White Paper came from another quarter. On March 11, 1935, Churchill vehemently attacked the statements made by the Prime Minister and the Under-Secretary of State for Air to the House in March, 1934. At that time they had stated that Britain "still had a margin of superiority over Germany in air strength and would at the end of 1935 still possess a margin of superiority." Churchill challenged these figures and warned that on April 1, when Germany officially was going to announce she had an air force, she would declare a figure of 600 first-line strength, and "it may easily be double or more than double." He stated that the estimates called for an increase of only 100 ships a year, whereas Germany, he said, would be producing 125 *a month*. He warned of the huge number of reserves she had in addition. He concluded by calling attention to the "geographical vulnerability" of London, and demanded that the Government remedy the situation.

This speech was not directly answered at the time. During the next two months the existence of a German Air Force was officially announced, and, in addition, Germany introduced conscription. Both of these actions had been clearly forbidden by the Versailles Treaty, but Hitler knew that no one either in France or England was ready to go to war about it.

In May, however, Baldwin answered Churchill's speech, and sought to explain why his figures of the previous year had been wrong. In defense of his previous statement that England would still be superior to Germany at the end of the current year, he argued that his figures of last November were correct, that he had been wrong only in his "estimate of the future." The reason for this was that "Germany's productive capacity had been misjudged."

In any discussion of Britain's rearmament efforts, the question always arises—why did the British leaders make these appalling mistakes in regard to Germany's output? Why did Baldwin, for example, make such an error in his calculations in 1934? Why did the British continue to make them in 1935 and 1936? These mistakes were fatal, as the British planned their own production in accordance with what they thought would be Germany's. Were they misinformed? Were they merely over-confident? Was their attention so concentrated on their immediate domestic concerns that they slept undisturbed by warlike preparations on the continent?

The truth is that Germany got a head start before the Allies grasped what she was about. This was accomplished not so much by the manufacture of actual implements of war, as by laying a foundation for their manufacture. The German locomotive industry, for example, was assigned to the manufacture of tanks instead of rolling stock for the deteriorating German railways. Germany was shrewd in getting tooled-up for aircraft production. It is apparent, from the discussion that has been going on in America in the last two months, that tools are the real "bottleneck" of aircraft production. They cannot be turned out in mass quantities, and they must be made by skilled workmen. Above all, it takes time to produce the number of tools required for great armament expansion. Therefore, it takes more than a year to get factories organized for the production of munitions on a large scale. Germany got the jump principally by *getting everything set for a large-scale output rather than by actual output itself*, though its output was considerable.

It is difficult to keep track of manufacturing in a

foreign country, especially in a country like Germany where all the preparations were guarded in totalitarian secrecy. It was possible, therefore, for the Allied leaders to overlook this preliminary preparation. During this period, it will be remembered, there was considerable talk in Germany about a new cheap car that would make an automobile available for everyone in the Reich. But it was almost impossible to discover whether an automobile plant was being tooled to produce engines for "the people's car" or to produce engines for planes. When Germany, therefore, decided to start turning out planes by mass production, her task was easy. Britain, on the other hand, having judged Germany's future potentialities by her previous production, was caught completely unprepared. She had to go through the preliminary "tooling-up" period, which cost her nearly two years.

Germany's advantage in regard to tools was not fully realized until 1936. In his speech, Baldwin credited most of the error in estimating German productive potentiality to the fact that if a dictatorship wants to increase its defenses, in contrast to a democracy, "it can do it in absolute secrecy."

In his plans for the future, Baldwin showed that the Government was still not aware of Germany's full productive capacity. In his speech he stated that

Hitler had indicated that his goal in the air was parity with France, which at that time possessed about 1500 first-line planes. This, he had stated, was necessary for German security. Baldwin announced that Britain would have the same goal and that "they would proceed to it with all the speed we can." Lord Londonderry announced in the House of Lords that by 1937 the R.A.F. would be composed of 1500 first-line aircraft, compared with 580 at present and the 840 that they had set as their figure the previous summer. They would form seventy-one new squadrons (852 planes) instead of the twenty-two (264 planes) under the present program for 1936–1937.

This program, of course, was impressive at first glance. England and Germany were then equal—each having about 600 first-line planes. Germany had announced that her goal was attainment of parity with France, therefore England had laid down a similar program. The great error was in failing to see that they had misjudged Germany's output once, and that they might conceivably do so again. Which was exactly what happened. However, at the time they felt there was no great cause for alarm. While the feeling in England was not as friendly to Germany as it had been in 1934, there were a great many who felt, now that Germany had succeeded in obtaining the "equality in armaments" for which she had been working for the last ten or twelve years, some sort of agreement could be worked out. There was also the realization that France could be counted on as an ally of England's, and the two countries had, between them, over three times as many planes as Germany—2000 to 600. And lastly, and most important, there was the public attitude in regard to armaments. Londonderry, in announcing the new program, said, "If the program I have announced proves insufficient, we will increase it, cost what it may in money or effort, and we believe that public opinion in this country will give us unhesitating support in doing so."

What, exactly, was public opinion on this question of rearmament? At the beginning of the year, the White Paper on Defense had been coldly received. The tone of Baldwin's speech defending it, made several days after it was announced, indicates this. His entire speech was one of apology for its size, and assurances that they would reduce the expenditures at the first possible opportunity. *The Economist* wrote an editorial strongly attacking the Paper. Rearmament, it declared, would not bring about security, and it expressed satisfaction that the program was no larger. Numerous political federations and councils throughout the country opposed it also. Groups, like the League of Nations Union, protested that it was a desertion of collective security; and others, like the National Peace Council, the National League of Young Liberals, the National Council of Evangelical Free Churches, were equally outspoken in their opposition.

In any discussion of groups opposed to rearmament, no list would be complete without including the completely pacifist wing of the Labour Party led by men like George Lansbury and Dick Shepherd. Though the number of people who supported their advocacy of complete and final abolition of all weapons of warfare was limited, yet their indirect influence was considerable.

As the year progressed, however, and Hitler announced his military breaches of Versailles, there began to be indications of a gradual shift. The Liberal Party, which in 1934 had opposed rearmament, now supported the May Defense program; not because it backed the Government's foreign policy, but "because they cannot agree that to increase our national armaments is necessarily inconsistent with our obligations under the collective peace system." Another indication of this gradual change may be found in a speech of Sir Bolton Eyres-Monsell to the 1900 Club.

In these last four years we have had to swim against a strong current of opinion. . . . This current of opinion has been forced by a band of almost fanatics who thought they could propitiate the gods of war by cutting the service estimates to the bone, and this fanatical propaganda has attracted to itself a great tributary of thought from people entirely uninstructed who, while passionately longing for peace and economy, have very wrongly thought, and have been taught in that manner. I am glad to think there has been a great change of opinion and heart in this great mass of uninstructed opinion. . . . Last year the Naval estimates were twenty per cent above what they were when I assumed office. By the end of this year the Government will have sanctioned 15 cruisers in four years, which is the best record attained in any four years since the war.

Public opinion may have been changing but the results of the much-discussed Peace Ballot indicate that it still had a long way to go before it could be said to be pro-armaments. The results of the ballot have been sneered at and publicly discounted by many responsible leaders. There seems little doubt that all of the questions were "loaded." The ballot was conducted under the auspices of pro-League groups, and Americans accustomed to the strict impartiality of the Gallup and other similar polls are bound to be struck by the wording of the questions. It was such that no realistic opinion based on actual conditions was expressed. The returns on the *Peace Ballot* were:

1. Should Great Britain remain a member of the League of Nations?

Yes—11,090,387
No—   355,883

2. Are you in favor of an all-round reduction of armaments by international agreement?
    Yes—10,470,489
    No—   862,775

3. Are you in favor of the all-round abolition of National military and naval aircraft by international agreement?
    Yes—9,533,558
    No—1,689,786

4. Should the manufacture and sale of armaments for private profit be prohibited by international agreement?
    Yes—10,417,329
    No—   775,415

5. Do you consider that, if a nation insists on attacking another, the other nations should combine to compel it to stop, (a) by economic and non-military measures?
       (b) if necessary, military measures?
    (a) Yes—10,027,608
        No—   635,074
    (b) Yes— 6,784,368
        No— 2,351,981

Whether or not the ballot was "misleading or inconclusive," it does show the effect that the words "League" and "Disarmament" had on the minds of the people. The people did not realize that being pro-League might mean going to war; rather they looked on the League as the means by which they would avoid it. This belief was not to change until after the Ethiopian experience, when it appeared that sanctions might drag Britain into a conflict with Italy.

But there is one clear indication of how the country felt about this whole question of armaments. The general election was to be held that summer, and from the tone of the election manifestoes of the different parties it is possible to judge the attitude of the voters. For, of course, the manifesto presented a program designed to appeal to the greatest numbers of the public. And an examination of these manifestoes shows *that not one party came out for rearmament*. "Instead, all of the parties claimed that they put their faith in collective security under the League," and the general tone was definitely against armaments.

The Labour Party, although it was for defense forces "necessary and consistent with our League membership," was against "competitive armaments." In all of its campaign speeches, its chief attacks were based on the failures of the National Government to disarm. The Liberals struck a similar vein, and even the candidates of the Conservative Party, which had introduced the new defense measures, were extremely reluctant to acknowledge it. As the Chairman of the Conservative Party pointed out: "It was frankly declared that the *gaps and deficiencies* in our Defense Forces must be made good, but at the same time any suspicion of provoking a new race in armaments was firmly repudiated. Emphasis was laid on the impossibility, in the light of our responsibilities, of a continuance of unilateral disarmament."

This tone is far from that of a party embarking on a vigorous armament policy.

In the election we find that the Conservatives held their position as the majority party. They did lose, however, some of the tremendous superiority they had held since 1931. In the election returns, the Conservative Party won 387 seats, which was a loss of 84. Their coalition with certain other smaller parties brought their total figure to 431. In the Opposition, Labour went from 52 seats to 154, and its coalition strength brought it to 184. It should be noted, that in reality the opposition group was considerably under-represented, as the actual number of votes was only 13,149,451 to 8,434,231.

The new National Government found the following men in important positions in regard to defense. In the Cabinet were Stanley Baldwin as Prime Minister; Neville Chamberlain as Chancellor of the Exchequer; Sir John Simon as Secretary for Home Affairs; Anthony Eden as Secretary for Foreign Affairs; A. Duff-Cooper as Secretary for War; Viscount

Swinton as Secretary of Air; and Sir Thomas Inskip as Minister for the Coordination of Defense.

As I stated before, 1935 was a tremendously important year in the story of Britain's rearmament policy. If England ever hoped to match Germany's war effort she had to begin at that time. Nineteen thirty-four had seen an indication that she was ready to start, but 1935 saw the program strongly delayed. It is true the program was increased somewhat, but there was no real feeling in the country that the problem of armaments was of vital import. Though I have stressed the attitude of the different parties towards armaments in their election manifestoes, actually this defense problem was only one of three or four issues, the greatest discussions being on questions of social and industrial policies.

Nineteen thirty-five, however, appears crucial only *as we look back*. As I have stated before, democracies which are fundamentally peaceful have to receive external stimuli to force them to rearm. They do not have a long-range point of view. Rather, they react to each separate circumstance after it occurs. But when preparation for war, in this day of mechanization, takes such an extensive period, they are always behind. If they are moved to action by an event, say, in 1935, it will be 1937 or 1938 before their program is complete. By that time, they may have been shocked again by some new development, but it will take several more years before they can meet the new threat. In this way, the dictatorship with its long-range policy can always keep ahead of a democracy. A dictatorship's leaders realize that ordinarily armaments are so repugnant to a democracy based on a capitalistic system—which means everything must be paid for from taxes—that it will get along on a minimum armament program. A democracy will merely try to counter-balance the menaces that are actually staring it in the face.

Now, as applied to England, the menace of Germany did not at that time appear to be overwhelming. Though she had announced the existence of an air force and conscription, the English air force was supposed to be its equal, and the French army with its long training was, naturally, far superior to the newer German army. Although some of the British leaders may have been worried, it would have been difficult to convince the people that there was any need for a serious program of rearmament. Any further increase in the armaments program would have appeared to be "war-mongering." We have seen that happen in our own country, as late as 1938 and 1939, and there is no doubt that with the strong pacifist and pro-League feeling in England at the time a much larger program would have been impossible.

The responsibility of the leaders in not realizing and explaining the potentialities of Germany is heavy. But the English people must bear their share of the responsibility as well. They had been warned. Churchill and others had pointed out to them the dangers that menaced the country. They knew the Government's air calculations had been startlingly wrong. They had their opportunity to register their disapproval at the polls that summer. They failed to do so. The failure of their leaders to grasp the true situation is grave enough, but the English public cannot be exonerated of their share of the responsibility. They gave the stamp of their approval to the policy which has brought them so near disaster.

In summing up the year 1935, there are several points that should be noted. A slow change was coming about. There was a gradual realization among the people that their defense forces were not adequate—though the words "not adequate" generally referred to England's inability to carry out her League obligations. It was not until the failure of the League to stop Italy in 1936 that there was to be a cry for unilateral rearmament. Germany was becoming more and more unpopular with the masses. This was not due so much to unilateral repudiation of Treaties as to the repugnance felt in England to the totalitarian nature of the regime.

The feeling was very similar to that in the United States during 1937 and 1938 when most of our opposition to Nazism was based on its injustices to its own people rather than on any potential menace which it might be to us. Like England's, ours was a detached criticism of a form of government, rather than a realistic grasp of the implications of that form of government on the welfare of the world. And this is not the sort of feeling that calls for building up armaments for defense, but rather for speeches pointing out how fortunate we are not to be living in Germany.

As the year drew to a close, there was a growing comprehension of Germany's potentialities as a menace to England herself. A Trade Union Congress resolution at Margate on October, 1935, declared that "the German Air Force is now admittedly larger than that of Great Britain." *The Economist,* on the other hand, was still favorable to making a deal with Hitler and said that his May 21 speech, "made an overwhelming impression of sincerity on the great majority of English minds." It also bitterly attacked Chamberlain for advocating expansion of the Navy and Air Forces at the Conservative Party Conference in October, in contrast to Baldwin who had spoken for the need of disarmament as well. "It is certainly a regrettable departure from British tradition, that the Chancellor of the Exchequer should be the fore-most advocate of the increase in expenditure of ar-maments, and it certainly will not help to promote national agreement on foreign policy if collective security is to be used for an excuse for unilateral rearmament by Great Britain." As for the people, while they wished to maintain equality with Ger-many in the air, they were confident that the united League forces of France and England, combined with Russia, made their position more than safe.

The Government took a slightly more serious view of the situation. It was resolved to keep even with Germany and they were confident that the flex-ibility of their program, which had been indicated by the increases made in May over the March esti-mates, would provide for this. This, combined with the feeling of confidence inspired by France, and the more friendly relationship engendered by the Anglo-German Naval Agreement of June, 1935, made them feel that their program was ample.

These factors all combined to produce a feeling of complacency, a luxury England could not afford. Where 1935 should have been the year for the laying of a base for rearmament, it was a period of post-ponement and adjustment.

PART TWO

Period of Rearmament Policy

NATIONAL DEFENSE EXPENDITURES OF THE WORLD

1931–1936

(In United States dollars)

	1931	1932	1933	1934	1935	1936
U. S.	707.6	667.8	540.3	710.0	911.7	964.9
France	694.8	509.2	678.8	582.7	623.8	716.4
Gr. Br.	449.9	426.1	455.5	480.6	595.6	846.9
Italy	272.0	270.6	241.2	263.7	778.1	870.8
U.S.S.R.	280.8	282.5	309.5	1000.	1640.	2963.1
Japan	131.8	199.1	253.1	271.9	296.2	307.2
Germany	246.8	253.5	299.5	381.8	2600.	2600.
European Total	2748.9	245.80	2690.7	3519.7	7083.7	8879.7
World's Total	4067.2	3815.7	3992.0	5064.1	8810.1	10730.7

Note: Figures in Germany range from 4,000,000 to 12,000,000 marks since 1933.

Source of figures: Foreign Policy Report—European Military Policies, May 1, 1936, Stone and Fisher.

1936

Feb. 16   Victory of the Popular Front (Republicans) at Spanish Election

Mar. 7   Reoccupation of the Rhineland

May 3   Victory of the Popular Front (Leon Blum's socialist coalition) in the French General Election

May 9   Italy annexes Ethiopia

July 4   The Withdrawal of Sanctions from Italy

July 17   Outbreak of the Spanish Civil War

Sept. 8-14 The Nuremberg Party Congress proclaims the Nazi Four-Year Plan and a world crusade against Bolshevism

VI

The Launching of the Rearmament Program, 1936

THE YEAR 1936 is really the beginning of the modern period. In the first place, it saw the end of the old British foreign policy based on the League of Nations. The sanctions fiasco, with its demonstration of the fundamental weakness of the League, marked the end of collective security, other than as an ideal. The German march into the Rhineland spelled the end of another cornerstone in the British scheme of security, the Pact of Locarno. These two events brought about a basic change in Britain's defensive position. From this time forward Britain's armaments were planned with the realization that there was no great world order to protect her. Now it was up to her directly. What effect did this have on the armaments program?

Let us look at the actual defense policy that was presented to Parliament in the yearly estimates submitted in March. It is interesting to compare this program to subsequent proposals put forth later in the summer, as the March estimates were drawn up before sanctions had proved a failure, and before Hitler remilitarized the Rhineland.

Winston Churchill, in a speech of October 24, 1935, had warned the Government that "eight hundred million pounds of sterling was being spent in currency in the present year on direct and indirect military preparations in Germany." He also stated that "We have no speedy prospect of equaling the German Air Force or of overtaking Germany in the air, whatever we may do in the near future."

It had by now become evident to most people in England that German rearmament could no longer be shrugged off, as Simon had done in 1934, as being simply a "desire for equality."

On March 11, the Government submitted its White Paper on Defense. The general tone is somewhat different from that of previous years. No longer is it apologetic; it is merely explanatory, indicating that the need for rearmament was far more generally recognized than previously. It first called attention to the steps taken by the rest of the world in rearming. The Paper then pointed out that Britain had no other alternative than "to provide the means both of safeguarding ourselves against aggression and of playing our part in the enforcement of international obligations."

That the Government was still not definitely convinced of the inevitability of armaments is shown by the statement that it would continue to discourage competition in armaments. It gave the recent Naval Agreement with Germany of June, 1935, and the negotiations then going on with the United States regarding naval limitations as instances. It admitted that a general raising of armament levels all around was no guarantee of peace. But, "In determining our own defense program, it is impossible to disregard the extent of the preparations of others." It warned, however, that the provisions of the Paper could and would be modified if the situation changed. This last statement indicates that the Government had by no means accepted the idea that a war with Germany was inevitable. This is an extremely important point and was to become more important during the next three years.

The British realized that they must make some efforts to build up their armaments. Yet to them war was such an unsatisfactory solution of the problems then confronting Europe that they could not make themselves believe that it was a serious and dangerous threat. In their eyes, the important problems in Europe were questions of trade and tariffs. They felt that the gravest errors that had been made at Versailles were economic rather than political. Even the question of colonies, they believed, could be worked out satisfactorily. To none of these problems would a war be a solution—it would only make them far worse.

They did not see the Nazi movement as a revolutionary movement, heading for European domination. Hitler's propaganda and speeches were so effective that they numbed any reaction that the British felt from the reintroduction of conscription or the invasion of the Rhineland. This had a vital effect on England's defensive effort. To prepare for a war today requires a nation's united effort. England's was bound to be only half-hearted, as she was not convinced that war was inevitable. She was not to get that united effort until Munich had shocked the people into an awareness of their vulnerability, and the invasion of Prague in March convinced them once and for all that a "deal" could not be made with Germany. Meanwhile, it is important to note, in studying the program for 1936, that the hope of an equitable solution with Germany was still very strong.

The actual estimates submitted called for a total expenditure of £158,211,000, although by the end of the year this figure amounted to £188,163,000. This is nearly double the figure of 1931 when we began the analysis—the expenditure has risen from

$449,900,000 to $846,900,000. It is also an increase of $250,000,000 over the previous year.

The Naval estimates totaled £69,930,000; this figure was to be supplemented in May by another £10,-000,000. This was an increase of £20,000,000 over the previous year, due to the scare given the Navy by Mussolini, when the Fleet in the Mediterranean found that many of their guns had ammunition for only one or two rounds.

I have pointed out that democracies require jolts to awaken them. England got her jolt in regard to the Navy in 1936. Thus, when the present war broke out, the British Navy was the one branch of the Services that could be said to be in excellent condition. During 1936, 1937, and 1938 England engaged in one of the most active building periods in her career, and it has served her in good stead in the present war.

The estimates for the Army were up about £6,-000,000 to £49,281,000, but the White Paper indicated the general attitude towards this branch, when it said that as the Army had "been reduced twenty-one battalions since 1914 . . . it was proposed to raise four battalions to mitigate the present difficulties of *policing duties.*"

As in 1935, the Air estimates witnessed the most substantial increase. They were nearly doubled, reaching the figure of £39,000,000 plus another £3,-000,000 allotted to the Fleet Air Armaments. The building program was once more "revised to keep abreast of changing circumstances." The number of planes planned for Home Defense (England) was now raised from the 1500, proposed in 1935, to 1750 and 144 planes were added to the Imperial Defense (the Empire).

In addition to the rise in the estimates, there were certain other innovations that marked the beginning of the present period. An Air Raid Precaution office was set up, and it was announced officially on March 13, that Sir Thomas Inskip had been appointed Minister for the Co-ordination of Defense. His job, while he had little actual authority, was to co-ordinate all the requirements of the different services and to act as liaison between them and industry.

The White Paper then announced the setting up of the now famous "shadow factory scheme." This idea was an attempt to meet the German productive capacity of planes, taking into consideration the differences between the two countries' industrial set-up. Briefly, the theory behind the shadow factories was that each factory should make certain airplane parts, which would be assembled at a certain plant. This, of course, was entirely different from the German and American organization in which the entire plane was produced at the same factory. The advantage of the British scheme lies in the fact that each of the other existing factories could manufacture the parts they were most suited to handle. The Government would give subsidies to certain big companies, like Austin Motors. They would then put in the necessary tools, and start in with *"educational"* orders. At the same time they could continue their usual business. Meanwhile, labor would be constantly shifted in the new department, so that all the employees would become skilled in airplane production. Then if and when the emergency came, the company could quickly change its whole production capacity into producing planes.

Because of England's industrial set-up, this scheme was peculiarly adapted to her requirements. The disadvantages of the scheme, however, are obvious. In the first place, it meant that it would be several years before they could get the whole system running smoothly. The continual shifts of labor would necessitate *"educational"* orders for a considerable period. Secondly, there was the danger that a swift air raid might put one or two key factories out of production. This might well tie up the entire system. Thirdly, there was bound to be a tremendous amount of inefficiency in assembling the planes. All the factories were new at their job. It was difficult at

the time to know how long it would take the factories to do their particular tasks, and it was difficult
to co-ordinate the shipping to the central point. The
result was that at different times the British found
themselves with hundreds of propellers and no engines, hundreds of engines and no fuselages, and
so on.

For the first two or three years, the inefficiency of
such a system was bound to be extensive. There is
no doubt that the German and American way of doing the entire job in one plant is more efficient. England's great engine manufacturer, Lord Nuffield, felt
this so strongly that he refused to take part in the
general scheme. Nevertheless, it was felt that this
was so much cheaper, and that it would interfere so
much less with the country's normal industrial life,
that it received general support throughout the
country. I have discussed this problem in some detail as it explains much of the subsequent inefficiency and delay in Britain's air progress.

After announcing this new industrial plan, the
White Paper cited the need for skilled labor in this
new type of production. It added that every precaution would be taken to ensure that profits would be
limited. The whole organization of the new defense
preparations indicate that the Government was be-

coming really serious about this problem. What was the reaction to it in Parliament?

The Labour Party continued to oppose rearmament. It was now in a position somewhat similar to that of the Conservative Party in 1934 and 1935. Then the public had been opposed to rearmament. Now the public was changing; armaments were regarded as necessities. In opposing them, Labour was standing against the tide of popular opinion. But its stand was predicated on the theory that "security cannot be achieved by competitive rearmament." It voted against the defense measures, as I have said before, because they were part of the Government's foreign policy. Their opposition was not, they carefully pointed out, because they felt Britain should continue to neglect her armaments. The truth was that Labour was becoming doubtful of its own position. A good portion of Labour's voting strength came from the Trades Unions, and the Trades Unions were not greatly opposed to armaments, which, they thought, would mean increased employment. This put the Parliamentary wing of the Labour Party in a difficult political position.

The Liberal Party, led by Sir Archibald Sinclair, the present Air Minister under Churchill, also opposed the Government. But this was not because they were against the idea of the Government's building up the defense forces, but rather because they opposed the particular way in which the Government was doing it. Sinclair stated, "Denunciation of any expenditure upon the modernization and equipment of the British land, naval, or air forces could only be justified in principle from the point of nonresisting pacifism."

Winston Churchill, in his attack on the Paper, took his usual position. He attacked it bitterly, warning of German rearmament, and the tremendous figures that the Germans were spending.

The reoccupation of the Rhineland several days after the Paper was submitted, of course, made most of the country support it. Sir Samuel Hoare's statement that German rearmament had become "the central factor in the European problem and the central problem of our defensive program," expressed the opinion of nearly all groups.

The exact extent of this German rearmament was a matter of great dispute in England at this time. What exactly were the Germans paying for their rearmaments? No budget figures had been released during the last year, so it was difficult to draw any definite conclusions. In addition, there was the great problem of having to figure amounts in Reichsmarks, which then had to be translated into pounds. As there were several values for the mark, the figures had little significance as far as "buying" power went.

In April, Winston Churchill gave the amounts spent for German rearmament since 1933 as £2,000,-000,000. This seems to have been an extreme figure. A series of articles in *The Banker* in 1937 placed the expenditures up to 1936 at around 18,000,000,000 Reichsmarks. At the par rate of twenty Reichsmarks to the pound the figure would be £900,000,000. At the then current fixed rate of exchange of twelve Reichsmarks to a pound, the figure would be £1,-500,000,000. A compromise between the two figures would place Germany's armament expenditure around £1,200,000,000, which is slightly more than half of Churchill's figure.

The Economist, in an article of August 1936, figured the German expenditure at about 24,000,000,-000 Reichsmarks. This translated into pounds would be either £1,200,000,000 or £2,000,000,000, according to whether you accepted the current or the par rate for the mark. A compromise would bring it to £1,600,000,000. A fourth source, an article in *The Spectator,* figures the amount spent as "15,000,000,-000 marks or £1,200,000,000." The Foreign Policy Association reports that the figures in Germany range from 4,000,000,000 to 12,000,000,000 Reichsmarks, up to April 1936.

I have cited these different authorities chiefly because they illustrate how difficult it was to judge
Germany's armed effort. I have pointed out before
that it was possible for the British Government to
make a mistake in its estimates of Germany's potential output, and these various opinions are cited to
show that there was no real and accurate knowledge
of how much rearmament was going on in Germany.

Not only was it impossible to get a consensus in
regard to the amount of money Germany was spending, but there was no agreement, in any group in
Parliament, on the number of planes Germany then
possessed. According to an article in *The Spectator,*
which would represent more neutral opinion, it was
thought that in April 1935, when they announced
their Air Force, Germany had 1000 first-line planes
and 300 reserves—a total of 1300. In 1936 they had a
total, roughly, of 2000. In April 1935 England had
about 600 first-line planes and a total of 1434 planes.
France had 1500 first-line planes and a total of 2286.
By 1936 England had in all about 1650 planes and
France remained at about the same figure as in 1935.
According to these figures, therefore, England and
France were still markedly superior in numbers to
Germany—about 4000 to 2000.

There were two great weaknesses, however, in
these figures. The first was that France, for the next

months, was to be under the Socialist Government of Léon Blum. She was to introduce a complete program of social legislation; she was to give birth to the idea of the sit-down strike; and she was to see her entire production system torn and thrown off gear. This, combined with France's industrial and general financial set-up, resulted in France's Air Force remaining at around the same figures. Plane production fell to almost nothing in the next two years.

As the years 1935, 1936, and 1937 saw a great development in plane structure and plane speeds, France's old models became outmoded and could no longer be considered first-line. The result was that in September, 1938, the French Air Force could be considered at best a dubious asset. France recognized this in 1939 and an expansion program, calling for 2600 first-line planes, was approved before the war, to be completed by April, 1940. It was due to her small output that France made a great effort to supplement her production by buying in the United States. The importance of all this in our discussion lies in the fact that much of England's program was planned with the expectation that the French Air Force could be counted on to supplement figures. When French production failed to materialize, English figures were thrown out of scale.

On the whole, in summing up the reactions to the

White Paper in March, and observing the general opinion expressed in articles, it may be said that those who still opposed rearmament were chiefly members of small organized minority groups. The country as a whole had been definitely converted to the need of rearmament. This conversion, which had begun in the Government in the fall of 1934, had not reached any great strength either in the people or the Government until the fall of 1935 and the winter of 1936.

A shattering of the ideal that was the League and the dawning realization of Germany's great productive capacity had now made the country ready for rearmament. But it was still a democracy, which was leisurely and confidently turning to rearmament, not a frightened and desperate nation. It was not a nation with a single purpose, with all its energies headed in one direction; this was not to come until after Munich. The fear for its national self-preservation had not become strong enough to cause groups to give up their personal interests for the greater national purpose. In other words, every group wanted rearmament, but no group felt that there was any necessity for sacrificing its privileged position.

The "City," or business group, was still unwilling to see great expenditures made on armaments. Both in England and in America there has always been a strong feeling against armaments as pump-priming, or as genuine stimuli to business. Several years ago when it appeared that a big armaments bill was to be presented to Congress, the United States Chamber of Commerce issued a resolution condemning armament expenditure as a method of increasing prosperity. It warned that expenditure of this sort should be purely on the grounds of military necessity. In December 1938, the Congress of American Industry passed a similar resolution. It said that any prosperity created by this type of expenditure was artificial and was only a temporary stimulant. Business in England felt this way, too, and therefore was opposed to any great armament program, as they realized that they would have to foot most of the bill. But it was not only among the business groups that we find this unwillingness to make great sacrifices.

In the White Paper, it had been suggested that industry and labor should get together in conversations, to try to work out the new program with a minimum of sacrifices on both sides. On its part, the Government had promised to abstain from applying any compulsion on either party. In an April speech, Churchill called attention to the fact that, although one month had passed, labor and industry had not as yet met together. In fact, although the employers had written to the Amalgamated Engineers Union, one of England's great trade unions, they had received no response for over five weeks. The reason for this was pointed out in a letter from the Secretary of the Union, to *The Times* on May 12. In it he set down what labor's general views were towards this question of co-operation. The Secretary's letter indicates the feelings that motivated the Trade Unions during this and the subsequent period. He pointed out the "false promises" that had been made to labor during the World War and stated that there were a number of unemployed among the skilled workers who should be given jobs before there was any dilution. "We remind Sir Thomas Inskip [the Minister for the Co-ordination of Defense] that what they were asking us to do was to open our industry to allow unskilled men to do skilled men's work."

In order to understand how horrified a Trade Union man was at the thought of opening "our industry to allow unskilled men to do skilled men's work," it is necessary to realize the position labor held in England. Labor is organized on far more rigid lines than it is in the United States. Although we have skilled and unskilled labor, our production is essentially mass production. English production is far more individualized. The average English product is the product of skilled workmen, men who have been doing their jobs all their lives and who love it as a craft. Before they were permitted to take their places in the union, they were obliged to serve a long period as an apprentice, a carry-over from the Middle Ages. That has given English workmen a pride in the standard of their work and of the work of their entire union, which they guard jealously. This fits in with the specialized nature of British production.

In the difference between a Rolls-Royce and a Ford, we can see the contrast between the two types of production. A Rolls-Royce engine is probably the finest motor built and it is essentially a hand-made product. The Ford motor, on the other hand, is the result of mass-production methods, highly developed. Where Rolls are turned out in single units, Ford can turn out his car by the thousands. This difference in the industrial organization has had a tremendous effect on later British plane production. English planes, like the Spitfire, have been acknowledged to be far superior to the German in workmanship and general construction. But, like Ford, the Germans have placed their emphasis on mass production. Their planes, though individually inferior, are turned out in such masses, that they have more than made up for the individual superiority of the British. In modern warfare, where the average life of a plane is figured at less than three months, the skill of the workmanship makes little difference.

For this reason, it would seem that the mass-production method is the better. Although the British have tried to convert their organization to that type, it has been a difficult struggle, and it has taken them a long time. Labor's attitude has been one of the great obstacles. Their unions were organized for the technical individualized production methods, and they hated to see their skilled labor diluted by men who were unskilled. In the first World War, they had agreed to it of necessity. They made great sacrifices; but when the war was over, they found that much of their old system was broken down. The new, unskilled labor that had been taken in could not be forced out. This resulted in a lowering of their standards, and they were anxious that this should not happen again. They were, therefore, wary of any plan that even faintly indicated more dilution. Consequently, the opposition of the Secretary is understandable.

Until British labor was convinced that the actual existence of the nation was threatened, they refused to co-operate. And as the Government itself did not feel in 1936 that the danger was imminent enough to require the use of force, nothing much was done. We have seen a somewhat similar situation in America, in the attempts to exempt labor from the limits of the Walsh-Healey Act, and to allow a forty-eight-hour week in the Navy Yards. This has been strongly opposed, as it was felt that it would mark the beginning of the conscription of labor in America. And until we feel vitally menaced, any such condition will continue to be strongly opposed. The unwillingness of labor in both countries to sacrifice what it has taken them years to build up because of a somewhat vague external menace, is the natural result of their having had to be continually on guard during the last years to protect what they had already gained. However, the Secretary's letter concluded on a note which showed that the Union was concerned with more than standards of labor.

In describing the Union's interview with Sir Thomas Inskip, the Secretary said, "We suggested that there was one thing that might be done which could be calculated to have the desired effect. We had a door to open which was depriving 300,000 people of work. This door would be thrown wide open *if you decided to send instruments of warfare to help the legally elected government of Spain in their struggle against Germany, Italy and France.*" This was a reference to the embargo on arms put on Spain by the British Government. The Trade Unions were strongly supporting the loyalist cause

and so were opposed to the embargo. But this drag-
ging of international politics into the domestic problem of rearmament illustrates the complexity of the
forces with which a democracy must contend in putting through a national endeavor, and it is important in contrasting the progress of German and British rearmament. In a totalitarian state, this issue
would never have arisen. This type of freedom is one
of the penalties of democracy, and the attitude of
placing group and political interests above the national interests was by no means confined to labor—
it was typical of all groups.

Another clear illustration of the difficulties a democracy must face in dealing with a problem as gigantic as the one England was now handling, is
shown in the debates over the Ministry of Supply.
These debates were to continue for three more years
and, in its stand on this problem we see a clear picture of the Government's attitude towards this whole
question of rearmament.

On May 21, in the Commons, Churchill rose and
demanded a Ministry of Supply to supplement the
Ministry of the Co-ordination of Defense. He said
that one minister could not co-ordinate the policies
of the three services on tactical lines and, in addition, handle the whole problem of their relation-
ships with industry. From Churchill's description of

what the functions of a Ministry of Supply should be, the Government felt that it would entail giving the Minister dictatorial powers, and this the Government was unwilling to do. Sir Thomas Inskip replied to Churchill for the Government. He said that the Government was unwilling to give any Ministry these dictatorial powers. "That is where the Government and my right honourable friend part company. . . . My right honourable friend would take the gigantic stride which would put a great part of our industrial system on a war basis. He has naturally been impressed with the example of thoroughness afforded by Germany. He has invited us to follow that example. His Majesty's Government up to now have taken a different course."

In a speech on May 29, in Parliament, Inskip repeated his statement and illustrated by examples how a Ministry of Supply, *unless it had dictatorial powers,* could accomplish "nothing that could not be done under the present system." The fundamentals of the issue were whether England should organize industry and labor on a wartime basis or not. The Government felt that their present system was the more effective, voluntary co-operation rather than industrial conscription. It was felt that the competition for labor and material was not between branches of the Army, Navy, and Air Force, but rather was between the Service requirements and those of civil industry. In order to settle the question of priority between these two, a complete system of control would have to be set up. This might well have meant a dislocation of trade budgets and the general financial and credit structure of the country. And after coming through the financial depression of 1929–1931, no one wanted to take that risk. It would also have had a great effect on England's export trade. If her export production was held up, she might well lose markets to competitors like the Japanese, and never be able to get them back.

More and more it was becoming apparent that upon the export trade would fall a great share of the burden if a war began. The only way England could hope to match Germany's rich, natural resources, was through her imports. If her export trade was cut down she would rapidly find herself obliged to sell her investments in other countries to pay for these vital raw materials. Then when her cash ran out, she would be finished. If, however, she kept her trade lanes open, she could continue to buy from America and other countries if war began. Her investments would still be intact and these, combined with the receipts from her export trade, would enable her to remain solvent, even though she would have to expend huge amounts.

The Government, therefore, preferred to interfere as little as possible with this vital trade. In order to have an efficient Ministry of Supply of the type favored by Churchill, it would need dictatorial powers and might throw industry out of gear. Until the nation was at war, or *knew it was heading for war,* it felt it would not be worth it. In addition, there was another reason put forward by Lord Halifax in November 1936, which gives us valuable insight into the later policy of appeasement. He stated that peace could be *attained by economic adjustments,* and therefore it would be defeating their purpose if they took steps to interfere with trade and make these economic adjustments more difficult.

It was this belief of Britain's leaders, that the reasons for the friction in Europe were reasons that could be worked out, which prevented her from taking steps that would have called for a complete change in the national life. If England *had known for sure* that she would be in a war in 1940, she would have put in departments like the Ministry of Supply. But to put them in for an indefinitely long period would have had too great an effect on the economic structure of the country to make it seem worth while.

This was the great advantage Hitler had over England. He could build his war machine and plan to have it ready to strike in a definite period of time. In the meanwhile he cared little what happened to the country's internal economy. He doubled, tripled, and quadrupled the internal debt but, due to the totalitarian nature of his regime, he was able to keep prices to a reasonable level.

Contrast this with England's position. England could not double, triple, and quadruple her debts or she would have gone bankrupt. She would not have been able to keep prices from skyrocketing unless she put in Government control, which would have marked the end of her as a capitalistic nation, and the end of her democratic form of government. The English were unwilling to risk this disaster back in 1936; in fact, it was not until May, 1940, that they gave the Government dictatorial powers equal to Hitler's. Meanwhile, however, Germany could expend sums of hundreds of millions of pounds a year building up for *Der Tag*. Britain realized that she could never match that effort year after year, and she was therefore unwilling to spend enormous sums until she felt that war was indeed inevitable. And this was not to come until March 1939, or indeed, with great sections of the country, until the following September.

The general problem of defense had now become of great importance to the House. Concern began to be felt generally with the progress being made. In May supplementary estimates had been submitted, totaling £19,752,700, of which the Air Force got £11,700,000. The total for the year had now reached £188,163,780. This figure did not, by any means, satisfy Churchill. He claimed that £800,000,000 a year was being spent in Germany, of which £300,-000,000 was for up-keep, the rest for "extraordinary expenditures and expansion." He then stated that England would be able to spend only £75,000,000 of her appropriation that year, due to the lack of facilities for production. In Commons on November 12, he again demanded a Ministry of Supply, and declared that, at the existing rate of expansion, the R.A.F. would not reach the promised 124 squadrons (1488 planes), in spite of Sir Samuel Hoare's statement that "the position is satisfactory." It was now becoming evident to all that Britain had started with her rearmament later than she should have. Churchill's speeches were causing some people to question why, for example, they were ordering machine tools, "which were the neck of the bottle," now, instead of a year before. Baldwin arose on November 12 to explain this failure.

The speech Baldwin delivered was one of the gravest political "boners" that any politician ever made. His "appalling frankness" has resulted in his being blamed for the entire condition of Britain's armaments. Although a master politician, he made the most elementary mistakes in phrasing, and from this time on he became the political scapegoat for Britain's failure to rearm. Much of what Baldwin said was true, but the manner in which he worded the truth made it appear that he had put his party's interest above the national interest, and that was fatal.

We started late and I want to say a word about the years the locusts have eaten. I want to speak to the House with the utmost frankness . . . I would remind the House that not once but on many occasions in speeches and in various places, when I have been advocating as far as I am able the democratic principle, *I have stated that a democracy is always two years behind the dictator.* I believe this to be true. It has been true in this case. I put before the whole House my own views with an appalling frankness. From 1933, I and all my friends, were all very worried about what was happening in Europe. You will remember at that time the Disarmament Conference was sitting in Geneva. You will remember at that time there was probably a stronger pacifist feeling running through this country than at any time since the War. I am speaking of 1934–1935. You will remember the election at Fulham in the autumn of 1933, when a seat which the National Government held was lost by about 7,000 votes on no issue but the pacifist. You will remember, perhaps, that the National Government candidate who made a most guarded reference to the question of defense was mobbed for it. That was the feeling in the country in 1933.

My position as the leader of a great party was not alto-gether a comfortable one. I asked myself what chance was there—when that feeling that was given expression to in Ful-ham was common throughout the country. What chance was there within the next two years of that feeling being so changed that the country would give a mandate for rearma-ment? Supposing I had gone to the country and said that Germany was rearming and that we must rearm, does any-body think that this pacific democracy would have rallied to that cry at that moment?

Up to this point Baldwin was on solid ground. Al-though many in England had forgotten the strength of the pacifist movement and the general feeling against disarmament, there is little doubt that he would have had an extremely difficult time building up a feeling for rearmament. But it was in his next few sentences that he made his great mistake:

I cannot think of anything that would have made the loss of the election from my point of view more certain. I think the country itself learned by certain events that took place during the winter of 1934–1935 what the perils might be to it. *All I did was to take a moment perhaps less unfortunate than another might have been, and we won the election by a large majority; but frankly I could conceive that we should at that time, by advocating certain courses, have been a great deal less successful.* We got from the country, with a large majority, a mandate for doing a thing that no one, twelve months before, would have believed possible.

It is my firm conviction that had the Government, with this great majority used the majority to do anything that

might be described as arming without a mandate—and they
did not do anything, except the slightly increased air program—for which they gave their reasons—had I taken such
action as Mr. Churchill desired me to take, it would have
defeated entirely the end I had in view. I may be wrong,
but I put that to the House as an explanation of my action
in that respect.

It is easy to see why this speech was so easy for
Baldwin's political opponents to take apart. It was
extremely simple to say that the reason for Britain's
not rearming was that Baldwin, as he had publicly
admitted, wanted to win an election.

It seems to me that this is making a political foot-
ball out of a poor choice of words. Baldwin, as his
friends and enemies alike admit, was an extremely
clever debater and political tactician. It is doubtful
whether he would ever have come out boldly in Parliament and admitted he had put his party's welfare
above his country's welfare. Rather, I think, he used
the general election as the best illustration of public
opinion at that time in regard to armaments. For an
election is, after all, the best barometer of popular
will in a democracy. However, in this speech, Baldwin does reveal his own complete lack of vision. He
admits he was "very worried" about what was happening in Europe. If this was true, it was unques-
tionably his duty to go to the country on that issue
and not on any other. For if Baldwin went to the

country on one issue in order "to gain a mandate" to support another, it puts him in the role of deceiving the public and playing politics with the country's welfare.

I believe, however, that Baldwin himself and his friends, although "worried," were by no means convinced of the need for rearmament. It should be remembered that in Baldwin's cabinet at the time were men of the type of Anthony Eden and Duff-Cooper, who were later to resign from Chamberlain's cabinet on questions of policy. It is doubtful whether Baldwin's entire cabinet would have supported him if they had believed any really serious cause for alarm existed. Baldwin should be condemned for his blindness and his unwillingness to face unpleasant facts, but I do not believe that he and his entire cabinet knowingly betrayed the country. They all made the mistake of misjudging Germany's potentialities and the Nazi psychology. This, combined with the strongly peaceful attitude of the people, explains why Britain did not start to rearm sooner.

I have gone into a discussion of Baldwin's speech at considerable length, as it is so often given to explain away the whole problem. It is only natural that Baldwin receives most of the blame. He was the Prime Minister during this period. But it would be oversimplification as the complete explanation. The

Conservative Party and the people had the opportunity in 1935 to register their disapproval of Baldwin. Churchill was pointing out the errors and they had alternatives. That they did not, means that the entire cabinet, the party, and the people must all share in varying degrees the responsibility.

The year 1936 witnessed the great change from a general psychology of disarmament to one of rearmament. It had been brought about by a variety of circumstances. Partly it was due to the weakening of confidence in the League, brought on by failure of sanctions. Partly because Germany was becoming more and more unpopular and was beginning to be looked on as a potential menace. And there was also the political factor. The Conservative Party seemed safely in the saddle for another seven years, so they did not feel as responsible to public opinion as in 1935. Even the Labour Party, because of pressure from the Trade Unions, had come around to supporting it. It was felt that the armaments boom would bring in more employment, and in addition they felt it was directed against Fascism, which had wrecked the Trade Union movements both in Italy and Germany.

To balance this, the feeling was very strong that arrangements could be worked out with Germany and

Italy in accordance with Neville Chamberlain's policy of appeasement.

The great change in regard to armaments had come about—from now on the question was not to be "Why rearmament?" but "Why not more rearmament?" And yet the feeling was only half-hearted. It was that of a man who, noticing that his suit is getting shabby, decides he had better order a new one. But, if he must choose between food or the new suit, a man will naturally take the food. England felt the need for armaments, but still preferred butter to guns. The fear of danger was not sufficient to compel them to relinquish their private liberties.

Let us look at 1937 and see whether the country was beginning to wake up to the seriousness of its position.

1 9 3 7

Jan. 2   "Gentleman's Agreement" (Britain and Italy)

Sept. 12-14 Conference of Mediterranean Powers at Nyon

Sept. 25-29 Visit of Mussolini to Germany

VII

Slowness of Fulfillment of the Program, 1937

ENGLAND'S ATTENTION was far removed from the questions of rearmament by the abdication of Edward VIII, late in December 1936. But it was brought back sharply by the "frank statement" of Sir Thomas Inskip on January 27, 1937.

We have seen that Britain's air program was increased as the situation grew worse. In November 1934, Baldwin had announced a plan that would call for 75 squadrons (900 planes) by 1938. The following March, due to the air activity in Germany, this figure was raised to 106½ squadrons (1278 planes). In May 1935, the program was increased to 1500 planes, as a result of Hitler's statement to Simon that his goal was parity with France. In March 1936, this figure was raised to 1750. This, instead of Baldwin's original estimate of 900, was now the goal.

Inskip delivered a full report on the progress Britain was making towards this figure. He said that 87 squadrons had been formed, thirteen of which were on a single-flight basis: that is, they were in the process of being developed. They were not as yet fully equipped and manned. By the end of March, he reported, they hoped to have 100 squadrons, twenty-two of which would be on a one-flight basis, and by July they hoped to have twenty more squadrons. Production of planes in the Austin plant would begin in the summer of 1938, and the shadow-factory scheme was progressing. However, in spite of his optimistic tone, it was evident that things were not going well. The program was not on schedule. An air program cannot be continually expanded except at terrific expense. The English planned their original organization of factories to produce about 1000 planes by 1938. Every time Hitler made a move they added several hundred planes to the production schedule. Unless enormous sums were voted for plant expansion, this type of expansion could not be kept up.

Churchill was quick to point out this condition. By changing the single-flight squadrons into their actual number of planes, he proved that by March 31 they would be forty-six squadrons (552 planes) short of the promised total of 1750. He then proceeded to figure out that the Germans now had nearly 2000 first-line planes and asserted that England had not one-half of this figure.

The White Paper and estimates submitted shortly after his speech showed that Britain was beginning to become really concerned about its armament effort. The combined gross estimates were £277,685,000, compared to the previous year's gross of £188,163,800. This is nearly three times the amount of the estimates of 1932.

The Navy estimates were up to £105,065,000, compared with the previous figure of £81,287,100, and the program of construction announced showed how strong had been the lesson of the previous year. The Army estimates totalled a gross £82,174,000, an increase of £26,292,000 over the previous year. And in the Air estimates there was also a considerable increase from £50,700,100 to £82,500,000. In relation to Germany's expenditure these figures were inconsiderable. In relation to England's previous efforts, however, they were a decided increase, and it was from the latter point of view, unfortunately, that most people viewed them.

The White Paper accompanying the estimates was entirely different from that of previous years. It was sharper and more to the point, all apologies and conciliatory statements were gone. It warned the country that, "Taking the program as it stands today, it would be imprudent to contemplate a total expenditure on defense during the next five years of much less than

£1,500,000,000," £300,000,000 of which would be raised by a loan. This was getting up into large figures. Britain's average yearly budget is less than £900,000,000 ($4,365,000,000).[1] The above figure would mean a yearly expenditure on armaments of £300,000,000, or nearly one-third of the national budget.

In comparing British armament figures with ours, it should be noted that the British figure represents a far greater per capita expenditure. In 1938, for example, the per capita expenditure in Britain was $44.00, that in the United States was only $7.00. The reason for this is that Britain has a far smaller population, and has a national income of around one-third of that of the United States. Thus, where an expenditure of, say, one billion dollars is only one-eighth of our total budget and one-seventieth of our total national income, a similar figure in England would represent about one-fifth of its budget and one-twenty-fifth of its national income. It would represent six times as much per capita. These facts must be considered in any discussion of the extent of the British armament effort. Thus, when the White Paper announced a figure of £1,500,000,000, or around $7,500,000,000, it called for a much greater sacrifice than an equal figure would in this country.

1 I have taken an arbitrary value of $4.85 for the pound.

What was the reaction to this great expenditure among the different parties?

The Labour Party met on March 3, decided to move "token reductions" to the fighting-service estimates when they came before the Commons. This meant that they would resist the estimates on the grounds of lack of co-ordination, bad foreign policy, and so forth, and that it would generally take the view that rearmament must be related to the whole questions of the League of Nations and collective security. When it came to the final questions of the service estimates, however, the Labour Party would abstain from voting.

That the Labour Party was torn in a number of conflicting directions can be seen in the speeches of its leaders. One branch was completely pacifistic: "It would refuse to fight, refuse to enlist, refuse to play at soldiering [e.g. the Territorials], refuse to be conscripted, refuse to vote for any candidate at any election who is in favor of war, militarism, or imperialism." On this line, an editorial in the *Labour Monthly* called upon the Labour Party to oppose the Government's armaments program instead of acquiescing in a "tacit understanding." It quoted Chamberlain's February 17 speech to the effect that it was "not in the public interest to set out a theory of whom we are going to fight or who might be our allies."

Though Chamberlain meant by this that there was no sense of breaking Europe up into two armed camps, this was not the editorial's interpretation. It said that merely confirmed their impression that there was no danger of any war. The armaments boom was simply being engendered by the capitalists for profit, and "Britain's rearmament is a weapon against labour."

Opposed to this group, who saw the entire situation from a purely Marxian point of view, was that wing of the Labour Party who, while completely opposed to the Government's foreign policy as being desertion of the League, were nevertheless unwilling to come out against rearmament. A dawning realization was coming to them that "force may be used by the dictatorships" and that some teeth must be put into the League.

Aside from this opposition to rearmament as part of the Government's foreign policy, there was among some groups great opposition to the armaments policy internally. This was based on the same feeling that was noticed in 1936. As the move towards armaments became more and more a national policy, the Trade Unions became more and more concerned. The threat of industrial conscription, which would strike at the very basis of trade unionism, was to them much more of a reality than the vague, more distant menace of Hitlerism. Nevertheless, when the problem was finally settled at the Trade Unions Congress, Labour admitted the need for rearmament. In a political resolution pointing out the need in England for a Labour Government, the Congress conceded, "Such a Government, until the change in the international situation caused by its advent had had its effect, would be unable to reverse the present program of Rearmament."

Although Labour thus agreed to the defense measures, there is no doubt that they opposed vigorously the idea that any of it would be financed by a loan. This, they felt, would bring on the danger of overproduction, which would be followed by inflation, which would mean higher prices. For this reason they took a firm stand against the Government's new Loan proposal as set forth in the White Paper.

The Government also got a certain amount of grudging support from another unexpected quarter. Churchill, in a speech on March 4, said he was glad to hear the amount of the sum that had been allocated. He warned, however, that it would be impossible to get very much of it circulated in the first year. This is a fact that is often overlooked. It is considered that if a huge sum of money is authorized, the job is done. But it takes time for contracts to be submitted and work to be completed. If a sum of money is voted in one year, it may take a year before it is completely allocated, and three years before the guns or ships or planes are ready, and meanwhile a dangerous and false sense of complacency may be produced.

Churchill concluded in a more optimistic tone. He pointed out that "Our Navy was far stronger relatively to any Navy in Europe than it was in 1914." And he called attention to the virtual "defensive alliance" between France and England.

The Liberal Party supported the rearmament program, as it had in 1936, and Sir Archibald Sinclair expressed its views when he said, "Every party in this country is resolved to support rearmament, much as we loathe it."

For the first time in England there seems complete unanimity in regard to rearmament, no matter what the views were on foreign policy. Whether the policy was isolation, collective security, or a combination of the two, rearmament fitted in with it and was necessary for its success. The great building boom in the Navy, the first line of defense, had made the people feel a bit more secure. But Lord Trenchard's speech of November 1936, in which he had pictured thousands of airplanes dropping in a few hours more bombs than were dropped during the entire last war, had struck a chill into the hearts of Londoners.

The theories of the Italian General Douhet, who described lightning knock-out raids, paralyzing a country at the outbreak, had seized upon the imagination of the British public. Books like Charlton's *War Over England,* with its gloomy picture of the horrors of London during an air raid, built up a feeling of terror of the air. The war in Spain, with its grim pictures of huddling refugees looking to the sky, added to this feeling. Emotions move people far more strongly than facts. And now the emotion of fear of death from the air began to seize the British public, and it was to have an overwhelming effect during the crisis of the next year. Yet, as though to prove that man is essentially, over a long period of time, reasonable, during the year after Munich this was to burn itself out. But it resulted, while it lasted, in bringing the country to a sharp realization of its vulnerability more quickly than all the logic of Churchill's arguments over the preceding three years.

The fear of this new type of war, in which there would be no differentiation between the civilian and the soldier, combined with a desire to build up its armaments, made Britain welcome the policy of the new Prime Minister.

On May 31, Neville Chamberlain succeeded Stanley Baldwin, who retired at the height of a great popularity brought on by the way he had handled the abdication crisis. In his acceptance address, Chamberlain announced the policy that was to become known as "appeasement." Appeasement to us now has a bad sound—it connotes Munich and backing down. In a vague way we blame it for much of Europe's present trouble, but there was more to it than that when Chamberlain announced it back in 1937. It was a double-barreled policy; he would "continue our program of the reestablishment of our defence forces, combined with a substantial effort to remove the causes which are delaying the return of confidence in Europe." That Chamberlain's policy was not merely an unsuccessful effort "to remove the causes delaying the return of confidence" is not popularly realized. It is the other part of his program, "continuing our program of the reestablishment of our defence forces," with which we are chiefly concerned.

Chamberlain's policy was motivated by two factors: he, first of all, honestly believed that some sort of solution could be worked out for Europe's problems. Having himself an essentially "business" mentality, he could not understand how any problems could possibly be settled by a war. Therefore, he felt that if some compromises were made so that the dictators would not be forced to go to war to save their popularity at home, Europe might have peace. In this he was wrong and it resulted in the failure of his policy.

At the same time, however, his policy was realistic, in that it was partly based on the knowledge that England, in 1937, was in very poor condition in regard to armaments. Her program was planned for completion in 1939 and 1940. He realized that war must be avoided until after that time at least, until Britain could build up her defenses sufficiently to prevent a knock-out blow. There is no doubt that Chamberlain made considerable efforts to build up England's armaments. At the same time, however, he had so much hope and confidence in his appeasement policy that he could not conceive of a war as being inevitable.

The result was that his energies were split. Although, in one sense, his two aims were harmonious, in another sense, they pulled in opposite directions. A boxer cannot work himself into proper psychological and physical condition for a fight that he seriously believes will never come off. It was the same way with England. She so hated the thought of war that she could not believe it was going to happen, and the appeasement policy gave her confidence that this hope had some basis.

There is no doubt, however, that Chamberlain proceeded vigorously to strengthen the defenses. On

September 20 at Geneva, Anthony Eden stated that there were 450,000 tons actually under construction for the British Navy. "Only on rare occasions in our history has a comparable naval effort been made." On November 4, Sir Thomas Inskip reported that, in the last eighteen months, orders had been placed for £288,000,000 worth of armaments, and announced that great steps had been taken towards developing industry along the necessary lines. And on December 3 the greatly publicized changes were made in the British Army to mechanize it in accordance with the recommendations made by Liddell-Hart. From this time on, it was also established that the Territorial Army, which corresponded somewhat to our National Guard, had "a claim on the same sources and standards of instruction as the Regular Army." This last statement showed that the army was beginning to be looked on as much more than the "police force" for the Empire it had been considered back in 1934 and 1935. It was also evident that the preparations were for more than merely filling the "gaps and deficiencies."

But that the need for defense was still not considered vital can be seen by the famous dispute over the Air Raid Precautions. The work on the A.R.P. had been practically stopped, due to questions about who was to foot the bill. The National Government felt that it should not pay more than seventy-five per cent, the local authorities were unwilling to bear any of the cost as they felt it was a job for the central Government. It seems now a trivial matter to hold up such a vital project, but nevertheless it delayed progress for many months. This freedom from centralized authoritarianism is one of the great cornerstones upon which democracy is based, yet in this case it was a definite disadvantage. Either the National Government should have paid the whole bill or they should have forced the local authorities to pay. Then a careful observance of democratic principles, combined with a desire for economy, produced a type of dispute that no nation can afford. That such a dispute could exist shows far more than mere statements what the attitude of the British was at this time.

So much for the section of Chamberlain's policy that called for the "reestablishment of our defence forces." The other part, the "removal of the causes which are delaying the return of confidence in Europe," was being carried on far more vigorously. In spite of Italy's withdrawal from the League and the difficulties arising out of the Spanish Civil War, the Government tried to lay the grounds for removal of "those causes." This policy received wide support throughout the country. There was real hope for the future. *The Economist* stated in an editorial: "There must be no slamming of doors upon claims which seem to the German people and to many others inherently reasonable." *The Times* wrote several leading articles, stating that if Germany could consent to the rule of international law, there was no reason why a solution to the world's problems could not be worked out.

The feeling in the country at this time seems to have been one of great general optimism, which caused Churchill caustically to remark, "I must say that I am astounded at the wave of optimism, of confidence, and even of complacency, which has swept over Parliament and public opinion. There is a veritable tide of feeling that all is well, that everything is being done in the right way, in the right measure, and in the right time."

The progress of the A.R.P. illustrates most clearly this general attitude. A sum of £20,000,000 was voted, which was to be spent *over the next four years*. In other words, England was not planning to complete her Air Raid Precautions until 1941. In the number of people who had volunteered for the A.R.P., we can get a clear picture of how the general public shared in this feeling of complacency. Of the total number of 1,000,000 workers which was the goal, only 200,000 had volunteered! And Germany, in 1936, had over 12,000,000 members in her comparable organization. As I have stated, the essence of democracy is voluntary action and co-operation. But you cannot get efficient voluntary action in a democracy unless people feel that sacrifices are essential. In the case of the A.R.P., Germany, by totalitarian methods, had worked out a much more satisfactory solution than had England. Yet, in a country like England where individual freedom was so highly regarded, no other method would have been acceptable. This is another of democracy's weaknesses which she must face in competing with a dictatorship.

In summing up the year 1937, the event of chief importance was the formal adoption of the Chamberlain policy for peace. England had entered 1937, arming for security, but without any one foreign policy. Realization of the failure of the League had made some men like Beaverbrook and Garvin favor an isolationist policy. Others wished to seek security through direct alliances, and still others were pacifists like Gertrude Russell, who felt it was impossible to defend the country against an air attack. The bomber would always get through. These groups still held on to their beliefs, but the country as a whole favored the Chamberlain policy of rearming and working for peace, as it was the most comprehensive. Appeasement meant different things to different people. To one group, it might mean being helpful for trade; to another, it might mean being anti-communist; to another, it might mean keeping out of war. Whatever it meant, it gave different groups a common purpose. It gave England a more definite feeling of unity than she had had for the last couple of years when she had been wallowing in a trough of indecision. It was the year 1938 that was to be the crucial one for Britain's new foreign policy.

In regard to rearmament, the effect of Chamberlain's policy was mixed. On the credit side was the fact that Chamberlain's policy of political appeasement was only a parallel one to the building up of strong armaments. Thus, extensive efforts were made to get on with the program. But the policy also had another effect which must be entered on the debit side. That was the feeling of confidence and hope that the appeasement policy brought to England. The effect of this was to give the people a false feeling of security, which was contagious and spread through all groups. The result was that people felt sacrifices were not necessary—"there isn't going to be

a war anyway"—and the achievement of that single-
ness of purpose, which is so difficult to acquire in a
democracy until moments of great danger, was postponed for yet another year.

1938

Feb. 13   Hitler-Schuschnigg Meeting at Berchtesgaden

Feb. 21   Resignation of Eden. Succeeded by Lord Halifax

Mar. 12   Hitler's Invasion and Conquest of Austria

Sept. 28   Munich

1939

Mar. 15   Hitler marches into Prague

Sept. 1   Hitler marches into Poland

Sept. 3   England and France declare war on Germany

VIII

The Penalty—Munich, 1938

Pre-Munich

How DEFINITE the new foreign policy had become was brought out forcefully when, on February 20, Eden resigned as Foreign Minister. The particular reason he gave for his resignation was his refusal to agree to continue the conversation that had been going on since February 1937, between Britain and Italy, until the Italian Government would "give some evidence of their sincerity" by "withdrawing a substantial number of volunteers" from Spain. However, the real reason, as he explained in his account to the House, was that he felt that "This was the moment for the country to stand firm, not to plunge into negotiations unprepared, with the full knowledge that the chief obstacle to their success has not been resolved."

Chamberlain said that this sentence described "the difference in outlook" between the two. "I was confident that his Government [the Italian Ambassador's] would approach the negotiations in the same spirit as we should do, namely in perfect good faith and with a sincere desire to reach agreement." In other words: was peace to be achieved by means of appeasement? or was it to be achieved by taking a firm stand?

Both policies had their disadvantages. America was much more sympathetic with Eden's; Americans believed it would bring an end to all these coups of the dictators. There was considerable feeling, both in England and America, that Hitler and Mussolini were just bluffing. Show strength and they will back down. This feeling was to provoke much of the criticism for the subsequent settlement at Munich. However, opposed to this was the fact that at that time England had not much strength to show anyone. Exactly how much was to be revealed nine months later at Munich. Many people in the British Government felt that, at that time, due to the need for continued triumphs at home, either one of the two dictators might prefer to "go down fighting." When one man can throw a country into a war, and the man is as emotional as Hitler, it would be a terrific risk to start any game of bluff. In addition, it was felt that to take sides definitely meant war between Italy and England "might become inevitable." And there was a strong hope in England that Italy would be won away from the axis. Whether right or wrong, this was the feeling among those who supported Chamberlain.

The reactions of the different parties to Eden's resignation are illuminating. Labour moved a vote of censure, indicating it supported Eden's policy. Its reason for supporting him was not that it was ready "to stand up and fight," but rather that it felt his policy indicated a return to security through the League. Churchill was more belligerent in his opposition to Chamberlain's policy. He supported a strong, active League policy and felt this had been abandoned in favor of bowing to the dictators.

The Dominions seemed to support Chamberlain's position, according to the statements of South Africa's Prime Minister, General Hertzog, and Australia's Prime Minister, Mr. J. A. Lyons. Articles in current periodicals such as the *Queen's Quarterly* indicate that Canada also supported it strongly. The French backed it in a statement made by the French Foreign Minister. But there is no doubt that it split the country, although the majority still favored Chamberlain's policy. The essence of this policy was stated once more in a speech on February 19. The Prime Minister said the Government's policy was, first, that England must seek to remove the causes of war; and second, make the country so strong that nobody would dare attack her.

Eden's resignation has been gone into at length, as it is here we find the essence of Chamberlain's policy and the policy opposed to it. One group thought that the only way to deal with the dictators was to show strength—the other felt that the way to get peace was to remove the causes of war. Their importance to this study lies in the fact that rearmament was such an integral part of both policies.

On March 2, a White Paper on defense was submitted. The tone of the Paper was entirely different from that of previous years, as the Paper proceeded upon the assumption, now almost universally accepted, that the "steps taken by his Majesty's Government are unavoidable, and that they furnish a steadying influence on the present state of international affairs." It declared that, while difficulties had been encountered, "the program has, on the whole, been satisfactory."

As far as the Navy went, the tonnage under construction had risen from 139,345 tons on January 1, 1935, to 547,014 on January 1, 1938. About sixty new warships were expected to be put into service during the year 1938. Among them were two new capital ships and one aircraft carrier. The gross Navy estimates were £123,707,000, an increase of £18,-642,000 over the £105,065,000 total of the previous year.

The gross Army estimates were up to £106,500,-000, an increase of £24,326,000 over the £82,174,000 of the previous year, and the White Paper reported that recruiting had been a record, "the strength of all ranks being increased 17,690." It also pointed out that "the majority of the units of the two anti-aircraft divisions have been provided with accommodations."

This last sentence indicates one of the great reasons for the failure of the British to have suitable anti-aircraft defenses during September 1938. It was because this branch of the service was regarded as being a special service tacked on to the Regular Army. Consequently, any money that was given to build up these units was felt to be money that legitimately should have gone to the Army proper for improvements. The Army at this time was busy trying to transform itself into a mechanized force, in order to keep abreast of recent modern developments. It felt that Home Defense was not its primary concern, and was, in fact, an unproductive drain on its purse. It, therefore, paid little attention to building up anti-aircraft units of defense. This task was put into the hands of the Territorials, who were regarded only as supplementary troops. This attitude had a great effect later on in the condition of the equipment and the number of guns. Because it was such a vital part of Britain's defenses, it should have been made a separate section, with its own appropriations from the start. Thus the Army heads also must bear their share of the responsibility for Britain's inadequate defenses.

The Air estimates were up to £93,500,000, an increase of £11,000,000 over the previous year's gross of £82,500,000. The White Paper reported that the strength of the Air Force had been raised in 1937 to 123 squadrons (1476 planes), the present force now comprised 58 bomber squadrons (696 planes), 15 squadrons (180 planes) of general reconnaissance aircraft, and 10 army co-operative squadrons (120 planes), in addition to the fighter squadrons.

The White Paper concluded by warning that the gross estimates for the five-year period would probably be over £1,500,000, which had been mentioned in 1937 as the sum that would have to be spent over that period. The total gross estimate for all the Services this particular year was £342,564,000, an increase of £64,879,000 over 1937–1938.

In discussing the estimates, Chamberlain gave the essence of the Government's policy towards rearmament, and indeed the whole British attitude towards war. The British believed very strongly, at that time, in Liddell-Hart's theory of limited warfare. It was so much more adapted to the country's geographic and economic position than any form of total war. It explains in a great measure why the British did not, until the very end, put much emphasis on building mechanical equipment. They always believed that the fleet would do their fighting for them. They knew that, in number, England, with a population of only one-half of Germany's, and with limited natural resources, could not hope to meet Hitler's efforts in preparing for war. But they felt there was no need to attempt this.

The Maginot Line was considered by everyone unbreakable. Hadn't the Allies pounded for a year at the Hindenburg Line in 1917 before they finally cracked it at terrific cost in men and materials? And wasn't the Maginot Line backed by the strong French Army, supposedly ten times stronger? The result would be a deadlock on the Western front, and meanwhile the British Fleet would establish a close blockade. England would then sit down and wait for an internal revolution to break out in Germany. Englishmen, with their emphasis on balanced budgets and sound economy, had watched the German financial hocus-pocus with amazement. Accustomed to the automatic laws of capitalism, they yearly prophesied inflation of the mark and the ruin of Germany's credit system. In addition, the repugnance that the British felt for the totalitarian nature of the regime made them think that no nation could possibly live for very long under such a system.

These ideas made them confident that a few months after the war began, especially if there was a deadlock, and the dictator could not keep adding easy triumphs, the people would rise and revolt. This was supposed to be democracy's great advantage: it could stand up under the pressure of adversity; it could always let off steam by changing its leaders without changing its system of government. In a dictatorship, a new regime could only be put in by a revolution, and the same discontent that resulted in peaceful changes in a democracy would blow up under the Nazi regime, because there were no safety valves for its escape.

Thus the British theory of war was that they merely had to build up their defenses to prevent a knock-out blow and then keep "business going as usual." Chamberlain expressed this view when he said in Commons:

The cornerstone of our defense policy must be the security of the United Kingdom. Our main strength lies in the resources of man power, productive capacity, and endurance of this country, and unless these can be maintained not only in peace but in the early stages of the war, when they will be the subject of continuous attack, our defeat will be certain, whatever might be the fate in secondary spheres elsewhere.

Therefore, our first main effort must have two main objectives—we must protect this country and we must preserve the trade routes upon which we depend for our food and raw materials.

Concern over the progress of rearmament was intensified by the annexation of Austria by Germany on March 11. Yet the debates indicate that there was still a considerable difference of opinion over how vital the problem had become and how real the menace.

Herbert Morrison (Labour), the present Minister of Supply, *warned of the danger to the social services* that lay in the Government's armament program. He felt that the huge sums being expended on armaments would result in a decrease in the amounts to be spent on health, relief, and so on. However, in their actual vote of opposition to the Government, the Labour Party explained its vote did not indicate opposition to rearmament but was only done because "we object to the general policy of the Government." Most of the party were now completely reconciled to rearmament but they wanted to register their disapproval of the Government's foreign policy, which they felt had, by its renunciation of collective security, caused the unsettled condition of the world which, the Government argued, necessitated the extensive armaments.

The Labour Party was, at this time, split on another aspect of the question of co-operating with the Government. The Prime Minister had repeated even more strongly the previous year's request that labor and industry get together. The Government still did not want to use compulsion, which would have meant industrial conscription. The Parliamentary wing of the Labour Party favored holding out for a change in foreign policy as the price for its co-operation. The Trade Unions Council, however, overrode them, as it wished to divorce the matter from politics or questions of foreign policy, and establish the co-operation on a purely industrial basis. In an editorial on March 26, *The Times* hailed the meeting which had taken place the previous day between the Trade Unions and Sir Thomas Inskip. It said the meeting represented a step further and beyond the idea of not interfering with the regular processes of industry, as it would give the Government complete priority, and yet there would be no compulsion. That the strife between the Government and the Unions was not completely settled, however, is indicated by the article in *The Economist* of April 9, 1938, in which it was stated that, while the Unions did not wish to impede National Defense, as long as engineers were unemployed or aircraft being exported (some aircraft had been sent to the Dominions), the Unions did not wish to repeat their war experience when rules and restrictions were not restored after the workers had co-operated with the Government.

In May of that year, for the first time, Parliament became aroused over the progress of the air program. So bitter did the attacks become that Viscount Swinton, who had been in charge of the program since 1935, was forced out of office. His place was taken by Sir Kingsley-Wood. The official explanation given was that it was felt necessary, in view of the great anxiety concerning this department, to have a minister in the House of Commons who could answer questions. As Viscount Swinton was a member of the House of Lords, he was by custom forbidden to appear on the floor in Commons, so there was no way for him to give an account to Commons.

In the debate that followed this change, Chamberlain admitted that there had been "delays, disappointments, and checks in the program, which has been altered from time to time, and expanded according to what we considered to be the need of the moment."

He described some of the difficulties that Viscount Swinton had encountered in trying to build up this new arm.[1] He had been forced to enlist the services of factories that had done no previous work of this type. At the same time, three basic changes came about in plane designing. These included the development of the all-metal monoplane, the design of new high-speed engines, and the invention of the variable-pitched propeller. These factors had all made Swinton's task more difficult but, according to Chamberlain, the fruits of his labors would be seen shortly.

He went on to discuss the problem of the Ministry of Supply [2] that Churchill was advocating, and described the machinery then existing. From his account, the Board at that time appears to have been similar to the Board recently set up by the President to handle the armaments problem in America. In regard to the question of giving the Board further powers, he said:

I submit to hon. Members that you can do a great deal today by persuasion, by voluntary effort, and by co-operation with labour and with employers; but if you want to produce the sort of effect you had in the Great War, *when the Government had absolute control over the whole of industry throughout the country, you must give this ministry the same sort of powers.*

We have had the same problem to meet in this

[1] Chamberlain's speech which is an illuminating account of the difficulties which arose is given in its entirety in the Appendix.
[2] See Appendix.

country: whether to give our recently set-up board the same powers that were held by Bernard Baruch's World War Board, or to try to meet the situation largely by voluntary co-operation. So far we have chosen the latter.

It is extremely dubious whether, in May, 1938, Chamberlain could have obtained support for measures that would have meant practically governmental control of industry. The recent insistence in America that men from industry handle the job of building up our own defenses, illustrates the opposition that an idea like this will receive in a country that is opposed to bureaucratic control. It is only when war is looked upon as inevitable, or when war begins, that such control will be accepted.

In his speech Chamberlain indicated that he realized this was no time to worry about programs, the job now was to try to produce as many planes as possible in the shortest period of time. Yet from his words we can see that he was still hopeful that his policy of appeasement would postpone any trouble for at least two more years. And the problem of air expansion was attacked with this in mind.

Viscount Swinton, in a debate on the Air Force Expansion Scheme in the House of Lords on May 12, 1938, promised a great increase in production in the succeeding years, but stated that it could be obtained only on one condition, *"and that is that the necessary labour is available."* [3]

There is no doubt that the problems Swinton faced were considerable. The Air expansion program came at a difficult transition period in plane development. There is no doubt that labor's attitude was definitely unco-operative. There is no doubt that the Government's foreign policy made all groups feel that there was no need for haste. There is no doubt that the shadow-factory scheme was very difficult to co-ordinate, but at the same time there were grave cases of inefficiency. Manufacturing was not co-ordinated; engines were turned out much faster than the other parts of the plane. The output of the existing factories was frequently not pushed to the limit, and the new factories that were often erected to take advantage of the boom were not always fully exploited. For example, one factory was put up at the suggestion of the Air Ministry and there it was ignored as far as orders were concerned. After several months of this, it was brought to the attention of a member of the War Office. He quickly got busy and in two weeks it was working on the construction of tanks.

Nevertheless although Swinton's ministry was not as efficient as it might have been, the lack of success of the Air program cannot be placed entirely on his

[3] See Appendix.

shoulders. It was a tartar for whoever took it, as the new Minister for Air, Sir Kingsley-Wood, who had an excellent reputation as an administrator, was shortly to find out.

What exactly was the position of the British Air Force at this time? How much progress had been made? According to a statement by Lord Winterton in the House of Lords, the Home Defense program "would have attained a first-line strength of approximately 2370 by March 1940."

It must be remembered, of course, that these are first-line plane figures and reserves must also be counted as the popular estimate at that time was one hundred per cent fatalities the first three months of the war. As Chamberlain pointed out, "air parity" does not necessarily mean equal first-line strength; many other factors had to be considered, such as reserves, potential wartime production, and the like. How do these figures shape up with what had been set down in the programs of 1935, 1936, and 1937? According to Sir Thomas Inskip's figures, the number of British planes in January 1937 was 1150, an increase of 300 over the figure of March, 1935. In other words Britain had increased her first-line strength at an average yearly rate of 150 or about twelve per month. In Germany, on the other hand, according to Churchill's figures of January 27, 1937, the increase in German Air strength between 1935 and 1937 was from a figure of 870 to 1800. This was an average increase of 500 a year or 41 a month. The figures for 1937 and 1938, however, indicate that Britain's production was improving as time went on.

In March 1938, Lt. Col. A. J. Muirhead, Parliamentary Under-Secretary for Air, figured Britain's first-line strength at around 1600, which would represent an increase over the 1937 figure of approximately 450 planes. That would indicate a rise in the monthly average from twelve to thirty-seven planes a month. And the figure of 3500 set for May 1940 would mean an increase to around ninety planes a month. These are very rough figures and do not give the true picture of the number of planes being produced, as there were, of course, continual replacements of old planes and considerable production of reserves and training planes. Nevertheless, it does indicate that, although production rose gradually, it was by no means mass production.

In connection with efforts to increase Britain's Air strength, Lord Winterton announced that Britain had sent a small mission to Canada and to the United States to investigate the possibilities of obtaining aircraft there. This is another reason why the Government was not more concerned with the Air situation. They always felt that they could supplement their production by purchases in the United States and Canada, if the situation became threatening. They were confident of peace for another two years, and they felt that there was sufficient time to get orders filled in America.

Yet, as the summer progressed, even the most optimistic could see that the international situation was growing worse. Germany was putting pressure on Czechoslovakia, and it began to appear as though England might be dragged into war through the back door. Although she had no direct alliance with any central European power, her ally France did, and England would have to support her. This growing tension accelerated the armament preparations.

To provide for the May expansion, a supplementary estimate was brought in, amounting to £22,-901,000, which brought the total of the year's supplementary estimates to £126,401,000, showing how considerable was the expansion of the program, as the international situation changed. On June 10, it was announced that the Government was buying 400 planes from the United States; and on July 15, it was stated that the Air Ministry had placed an order for 1000 Spitfires (at that time, the world's fastest military airplane). A feeling of anxiety pervaded all groups. Even *The Economist* had switched completely from its policy of minimizing the importance of rearmament and had become one of the Government's keenest critics for failure to proceed with rearmament moves vigorously. Publications can change their policy overnight, but it takes years to build up armaments.

That the situation in this summer before Munich was still regarded with serenity was demonstrated at a private meeting of the executive representatives of the joint engineering trades movement. The members ranged themselves alongside the Amalgamated Engineering Union, agreeing that "there was no justification for retarding existing regulations or working conditions." And Munich was only two months away!

Munich

The slow change from a psychology of disarmament to one of rearmament has been traced. We have seen that until after the year 1935 rearmament, beyond a certain limited point, would have meant warmongering to England and that the people would have voted a government supporting it out of office. We have seen how rearmament began in 1936 and some of the difficulties with which it was faced. Some came from natural causes; some came from poor judgment; others came from the placing of private group interests above that of the national interest. The nation had failed to realize that if it hoped to compete successfully with a dictatorship on an equal plane, it would have to renounce temporarily its democratic privileges. All of its energies would have to be molded in one direction, just as all the energies of Germany had been molded since 1933. It meant voluntary totalitarianism, because, after all, the essence of a totalitarian state is that the national purpose will not permit group interest to interfere with its fulfillment. But there was nothing in 1936 or in 1937 that caused the people to feel that the situation warranted allowing themselves to be regimented. No government could have convinced them; it was to take the fear of September 1938 to awaken them to the dangers of their position.

The potential power and destructiveness of the German Air Fleet was to bring home, through the fear it inspired, the comparative weakness of Britain as no amount of words or logic by Churchill had been able to do. England was in the same psychological position that we were in before last May. Then the potential menace of Germany awoke all groups in this country to the need for swift and intensive action. But no amount of facts and figures of German mechanized strength could have convinced this country as quickly as did the radio bulletins telling hourly of the new position of the advancing German armies. But, as it took this great shock to awaken America, it was to take a comparable shock to awaken the British people and the British Government.

For unwillingness to face the facts was not confined to the people alone—the Government too was not fully aware of the danger. It realized, however, that not only was Britain's strength not consonant with her obligations to her Dominions, it was not even sufficient to defend the island itself. It realized that it would take time to build up England's strength.

The policy of appeasement, while it was partly based on a sincere belief that a permanent basis could be built for peace, was also formulated on the realization that Britain's defense program, due to its tardiness in getting started, would not come to harvest until 1939. Munich was to be the price she had to pay for this year of grace.

The settlement of Munich has been criticized violently—nowhere more violently than in America. This was due partly to our realization that it was essentially a triumph for Hitler. That it should have been hailed as "Peace in our time," and "Peace with honor," appeared to many in America extremely short-sighted, to say the least. Chamberlain was accused of everything from being an arch knave who had planned the entire maneuver in May, to a dod-

dering old man who had been completely taken in.
The cloud of bitterness that swept over America has
prevented many of us from seeing the settlement in
a true light.

The great trouble was that few could think of
England except as the Mighty Britain of the nineteenth century. The truth has been brought home
sharply in the last year. The fact remains that in
1938, while Britain may have remained as strong as
ever, other countries had grown up who could challenge her, who could split her efforts. Japan, formerly
a weak power, could defeat her in the Far East, as
England could not afford to transfer her entire Fleet
from European waters. Four-fifths of the British
Fleet had not been able to cow Italy in 1935. Britain's
power had been based on her Naval strength, but
the importance of naval power had been changed by
he airplane. Coupled with those inevitable disadvantages was the factor we have been discussing—the
failure of Britain to rearm.

People in America, filled with the myth of Britain's
invincibility through the centuries, could not understand Chamberlain's desperate efforts to avert a war.
They felt, and many still do feel, that Hitler in 1938
was merely bluffing. "Just show him some strength
and he will back down quickly enough." Many in
England shared this belief, even in August 1939.

These people felt Chamberlain was badly taken in, but I think a study of the position of the two countries will show that Chamberlain could not have fought, even if he had wanted to. I do not claim that Munich was simply the result of Britain's inability to fight, as set forth by Baron Von Neurath. I believe Chamberlain was sincere in thinking that a great step had been taken towards healing one of Europe's fever sores. I believe that English public opinion was not sufficiently aroused to back him in a war. Most people in England felt, "It's not worth a war to prevent the Sudeten Germans from going back to Germany." They failed at that time to see the larger issue, involving the domination of Europe. But though all these factors played a part in the settlement at Munich, I feel that Munich was inevitable on the grounds of lack of armaments alone.

Let us look at the situation as it was regarded in Britain in September. Let us examine some of the facts that Chamberlain had to consider, before determining what should have been his decision.

A clear picture of the military factors that were considered can be seen in a Memorandum by Liddell-Hart, drawn up on September 2, 1938, nearly one month *before* the crisis. This Memorandum was the work of one of Britain's foremost military experts, a man who was very close to the War Ministry at the time, and who was later considered "anti-Munich."

In this September 2 Memorandum, Hart discussed what was to be expected if a war should break out over Czechoslovakia. He analyzed the Czechoslovakian position and concluded, "that the Czechs could not possibly hold out unless Russia could keep them from being dominated from the air." Could Russia do this? According to all the reports that the British had received, the Russian Air Force was in an extremely poor condition. Though larger in number, the technical inefficiency was reported to be extreme. This opinion was supplemented by the now famous Lindbergh report, which later proved to have been remarkably accurate. In addition to disclosing the tremendous strength and productive capacity of Germany, it showed that the strength of the Russian Air Force had been greatly exaggerated. Coupled with this was the question of her ability to come to Czechoslovakia's aid. Even if Russia had been willing, it would have been extremely difficult for her, as she was 600 miles away from any possible targets. In addition, Poland and Rumania refused unconditionally to permit Red Troops to cross their frontiers, making it geographically impossible for Russia to send infantry aid.

Furthermore, during the week before the crisis, when the Czechs were exchanging military information with England and France concerning the planes the latter would send in case of war, Russia refused to give any indication of her intentions regarding the sending of air assistance. Thus, if successful resistance by the Czechs depended on Russia's assistance, as Liddell-Hart had stated in his Memorandum, it left them small hope for survival.

Most experts at that time regarded the French Army and the German Army as checkmates, neither force daring to attack due to the fact that, under modern conditions of warfare, the experts at that time figured it would take three times as many men for the offensive as for the defensive. Although the West Wall had not been completed, the French scarcely had the necessary equipment for an invasion. Her whole theory of warfare under Gamelin was a defensive war behind the Maginot Line. The only decision could, therefore, have come from the air.

The figures on Germany's air strength varied— some guessed as high as 8000 first-line planes. Hart felt that at this time Germany had at least 3300 first-line planes, with great reserves of crews and machinery. The British had about one-half as many. More important, though, was the fact that at that time British production was only one-half of Germany's monthly output of 600. And as fatalities were figured at one hundred per cent the first three months of the war, this situation was extremely serious. Also the British factories were chiefly converted automobile or engine factories. They were naturally laid out in industrial centers, and they would have been easy targets for bombs. The Germans, on the other hand, had built their factories completely for plane production and with war in mind. They were situated far from the frontier and many of them were underground. In addition, France could not be counted on for much assistance. She had about the same number of planes as the English: 1500, but most of them would not go over 150 m.p.h. and their rate of production, due to labor troubles, hangovers from the Blum Socialist Government, was less than fifty planes a month.

What did England have in the way of bombers? Out of 60 squadrons (720 planes) of bombers—none of them was well organized and only about 200 planes were ready for active duty. As for fighters, on which the defense depended, the idea had always been, ever since Baldwin's speech, that "the bomber would always get through"—so the ratio of fighter to bomber was only 1:2. This was subsequently changed to 3:5 later in the year.

In regard to anti-aircraft defense, London had only seven of the 400 3.7 guns it had been estimated were necessary. Of the 30,000 volunteers needed for auxiliary fire-fighting service, only 4200 had volunteered by September 24, and only 800 of the needed 5000 women were enrolled for driving ambulances and fire trucks.

This was not all. According to Hart, and he was supported by other experts, the 1500 German bombers could have dropped 2000 tons of bombs a day on London. An idea can be had of the horror this caused when it is remembered that the Germans dropped only 74 tons of bombs on London in the last war, killing 851, and wounding 2058, and doing material damage to the extent of £1,400,000. On this basis it was figured that there would be 250,-000 casualties and £100,000,000 of damage the first week. Though these figures may look enormous, it must be remembered that they came from a cool, keen, military strategist who was very close to the War Office.

Therefore, the statement made by Bernard Baruch, former Chairman of the War Industrial Board, in commenting on the Munich Pact on his return from Europe, is essentially true. He stated that the Munich Pact was due solely to the unpreparedness of Great Britain and France. "Mr. Hitler knew that England and France were not prepared to come to grips at this time. He was ready to move and they were not. We ought to defend ourselves and our homes, and not find ourselves in the position of England at Munich. If England had been ready it would have been a different story."

In this book, I have tried to show why England was not ready. England's plan for war, as Chamberlain and others had set it down, was to build up her defenses sufficiently to prevent a knock-out blow, and then, because of her greater war potential due to her Empire, she would sit back behind her Navy and wait for Germany to explode or be blockaded into submission. If Chamberlain had fought in 1938, he would have been playing into Hitler's hands. Hitler had launched his rearmament program in 1933. England had launched hers in 1935 and 1936. Germany was organized on a totalitarian basis; her one aim was to build herself back to strength.

It is true that Hitler had started from scratch, but, with the great change in methods of warfare, this could hardly be called a disadvantage. Rather it cleared the path for complete mechanization and gave the German Army a far more modern outlook. Hitler's strength was naturally not as great as it was to be in the next year. For example, his stock of oil in 1938 was extremely limited. And in 1939, Russia was to be on his side. Nevertheless, the British were relatively far worse off in 1938 than they were in 1939. Their program, which had started late, was not planned to come to a head until 1939 and 1940. In addition, a great psychological change was to come about in England after the fateful days of September, that was to result in a tremendous increase in armament production.

Taking all these factors into consideration, the Munich Pact appears in a different light from that of a doddering old man being completely "taken in." It shows that appeasement did have some realism; it was the inevitable result of conditions that permitted no other decision. At that time, Italy was closely allied with Germany—no one knew which way she would go. Spain, with General Franco and his debt to the axis, was also considered on the debit side, according to Hart. And furthermore, Canada and Australia had both sent notes in which they stated that something could be said on behalf of the Sudeten Germans and that *they could not support Britain in a war.* South Africa was definitely opposed to a war over this question. The fact that a shift of around twelve votes in her Parliament in September 1939 would have kept her out of the present struggle illustrates how strong was the feeling there against war. People often forget that the British dominions are free and equal. They are at liberty to decide whether or not they are to go to war; and as it is upon their voluntary support that Britain rests her hope of victory, she is bound to respect their opinions. As Germany could have seized Czecho-slovakia and then remained on the defensive in the West, it is hard to see how Chamberlain, with his own defenses completely down, in addition to other factors, such as the state of public opinion, could have done other than he did at Munich.

His action on returning home gives the best indication of exactly how he saw the situation. Baron Von Neurath gave a good Nazi's opinion of how Chamberlain had been "taken in," when he called England's peaceful attitude at Munich the result of being "unable to embark on a European War at that time."

The criticism directed against Munich could have been directed with more accuracy against Britain's tardiness in rearming rather than against the pact itself. I feel that Chamberlain is to be condemned more as a member of the Baldwin cabinet, which had done so little to wake up the country, or for his own pre-Munich and post-Munich failure to bring to the country the realization of the great dangers with which it was faced, than for the part he played at Munich, for which he was so bitterly attacked in America.

The settlement of Munich was to have a tremendous effect on subsequent British armament effort.

The scare that had been thrown into the people by the threat of overwhelming air raids convinced them that they must be ready to make personal sacrifices to build Britain's strength. And the scare that had been thrown into the Government, when the reports started to come in from the different departments about their inability to meet the situation, convinced it that much greater efforts would have to be made than ever before. The activity of the next few months best indicates the effects of Munich.

IX

The Aftermath—Britain Awakens

THIS BOOK has been concerned with the problem of why Britain did not start on her armaments program sooner, and why, once it had started, it did not produce better results. Britain had been asleep, as far as a realization of the dangers that were facing her was concerned, and this produced fatal results in the fulfillment of her program. This period, which can definitely be called the sleeping period, came to an end at Munich. Munich brought its lessons home to the Services, the Government, and the people. There was now no excuse for anyone in Britain to regard the situation with satisfaction.

England had had a diplomatic defeat. Her prestige throughout the world had been dealt a terrific blow. This was realized, and the energy with which England attacked the problem was in great contrast to her previous lackadaisical methods. At the same time, however, the Munich experience had a debit side. Britain had come tremendously close to war. In the two or three days preceding Munich the people had believed war was inevitable. And then, it seemed almost miraculously, the threat was removed; there was to be "peace in our time." Many people in England who had seen war almost upon them, and then had seen it recede, believed that war now would never come. Another miracle would prevent it. This feeling was strong in England during the next year. The people hated war so much, they realized now more strongly than ever what it would mean to England and her position in the world, that they could not bring themselves to face its inevitability.

Thus there were two ideas working in England from September 28, 1938, to September 3, 1939. One was a firm determination to build up her strength, and the other was a feeling that England might now have peace. Maybe Hitler would be satisfied; maybe he was merely bluffing; maybe he really meant it when he said this was his last territorial claim in Europe. We can see the effect of these feelings during the following months.

Chamberlain's actions on returning home reveal that he had not been completely misled into believing that he could count definitely on "Peace in our time." In Parliament, in his homecoming speech, the Prime Minister said, "Because we have signed this agreement between these four powers at Munich, *we cannot afford to relax our efforts in regard to re-armament at this moment.* Disarmament on the part of this country can never be unilateral again. *We have tried that once, and we very nearly brought ourselves to disaster.*" His efforts to build up rearmament were at once attacked as being opposed to the whole theory of the Munich settlement. On October 6, he attempted to reconcile the two policies:

I am told that the policy which I have tried to describe is inconsistent with the continuance, and much more, inconsistent with the acceleration of our present program of arms. [The policy he is referring to is the policy of "discussion to get rid of the causes of war."] I am asked how I can reconcile an appeal to the country to support the continuance of this program with the words which I used when I came back from Munich the other day and spoke of my belief that we might have peace for a time.

Our past experience has shown us only too clearly that weakness in armed strength means weakness in diplomacy, and if we want to secure lasting peace I realize that diplomacy cannot be effective unless the consciousness exists, not here alone, but elsewhere, that behind the diplomacy is the strength to give effect to it.

One good thing, at any rate, has come out of the emergency through which we have passed. It has thrown a vivid light upon our preparations for defense, on their strength and on their weakness. I should not think we were doing our duty if we had not already ordered that a prompt and thorough inquiry should be made to cover the whole of our preparations, military and civil, in order to see, in the light of what has happened during these hectic days, what further steps may be necessary to make good our deficiencies in the shortest possible time.

The speeches made at this time are too numerous to go into except to indicate that *all* of them stressed the need for rearmament. No matter whether they were pro-appeasement or against it, invariably the need for vigorous rearmament was referred to. The great deficiencies that were shown to have existed, such as lack of anti-aircraft guns or lack of A.R.P. facilities, had awakened everyone to Britain's condition. Steps were immediately taken to correct them. The vigor of these steps was indicated on October 10 by Hitler's speech at Saarbrücken, in which he attacked Churchill, Eden, and others as "warmongers," and strongly warned England about her sudden armament spurt.

Another illustration of the confidence with which Britain had faced the future in 1936 and 1937 was shown in Chamberlain's speech describing the time when the program was due to be completed:

I want hon. members *to remember that our program of rearmament is a five-year program.* To argue that because anything has not been completed in the third year the program had broken down is to lose sight altogether of the fact that it was only intended to be completed in five years. I doubt whether it would have been possible if we had endeavored to do so to squeeze a five-year program into three years.

In November, Sir Kingsley-Wood gave an indication of what effect the Czech crisis had had on the position of the Air Force in the British defense plan. He announced that where the Air estimates for this year were £120,000,000, the next year they would total £200,000,000. The total number of fighter aircraft on order, or to be ordered, was now between 5000 and 6000. The program of 1750 aircraft would be achieved by the end of March 1939. Commenting on the program of May 1938, which called for a Home Defense force of 2370 planes and an overseas strength of 500 for 1940, he pointed out that the October output was fifty-one per cent over last May, and that next May would show an increase of 150 per cent.

The Army, too, came in for its share of reforms. In October Hoare-Belisha announced a reorganization plan for the Army, and said that the anti-aircraft personnel would be four times as much next year as it was last year.

The White Paper issue in February 1939 gives a clear picture of the great activity that was now taking place in Britain's armament methods. It called for a total defense expenditure of £580,000,000. Naval construction, it announced, had increased from

130,000 tons on January 1 to 695,000 tons on March 31, 1939. The Navy gross estimates totaled £148,-000,000, as compared to £123,700,000, an increase of £24,300,000 over 1937–1938. The Army's gross estimates were £148,155,000, an increase of £41,655,-000 over the figure of £106,500,000 of the previous year. The estimates of the Air amounted to £208,-561,000, an increase of £105,061,000 over that of the previous year. In his speech introducing the estimates, Kingsley-Wood stated that in November he had said the output of aircraft in May of this year should show an increase of 150 per cent over the output of May of last year. "We have achieved that 150 per cent increase." He then stated that the output of planes during 1939 would be 400 per cent over that of 1938.

In general, therefore, it can be seen that the country was making real progress. By the first part of 1939, the 1,000,000 workers sought for the A.R.P. had volunteered. Air-raid shelters were distributed in sufficient quantities to protect 10,000,000 people. Evacuation plans were completed, 40,000,000 gas masks were provided and a separate ministry was set up for civilian defense.

And yet, at the time these steps were going forward, we note the same reluctance to make sacrifices that had been so costly previous to Munich. As

believers in a democratic system, we have always had
faith in its innate powers of resistance. We believe
that it will be able to adapt itself to circumstances
and, because it is a system based on a respect for the
rights of the individual, in the long run it will prove
superior. We concede that a dictatorship does have
great advantages. We concede that the regimentation and the unification achieved by force and propaganda will give a dictator an initial jump on his
opponents. However, we believe that a democracy
can, by voluntary action, equal this effort when the
emergency comes and sustain it over a longer period
of time. We believe that groups will co-ordinate their
private interests with national interest, thus giving
a greater force and vigor than could have been attained by totalitarian methods. And in this we are
essentially right. The attitude of grim determination
that has characterized the resistance and efforts of
Britain through a series of disasters during the last
months shows the fundamental vitality inherent in
the system.

But the great difficulty is that the very factors that
contribute to a democracy's strength contribute also
to its weaknesses. The vitality and vigor, for example, with which labor in England has tackled the
problem during the last months in an effort to rebuild British equipment is possible only because of

the vitality and vigor which have existed deep in the Trade Unions system. And yet this same independent spirit resulted in their refusing to allow the Government to apply any methods of conscription before the war. With its knowledge of Fascism as the deadly opponent of Trade Unions, it has always regarded any pressure by the Government as a Trojan Horse that would lead inevitably to the destruction of labor's right of independence. And, until the last few months, this threat appeared even stronger than that of Hitler. With the basic feeling that Britain would always muddle through, that her Navy would protect her, labor failed to realize what sacrifices would have to be made. Though it takes years to build up armaments, labor was willing to co-operate only when Hitler was at England's very door.

This does not mean that labor is entirely to blame for Britain's lack of preparation. The Government and business were equally short-sighted. I cite this instance because it contains an important illustration of the problems with which a democracy must be faced when dealing with a modern defense program. To learn the whys and wherefores of British armaments, it is necessary to investigate *every* group—all must be prepared to bear their share of the responsibility. Chamberlain's Government will ultimately be held responsible because they were in office. And, in general, they should be held responsible. But it does not solve the problem to assign the blame to any one group. I have tried to discuss some of the factors that the country faced, and to explain the reasons for the leaders' decisions. It is easy enough to see now that they failed, but it is of much greater importance to understand why they failed.

To have a balanced picture, it is essential to emphasize the failure of different groups, as well as of the leaders of the Government. The question has come up again and again, as the great increase in production has been made by the recent great sacrifices of labor in England—why wasn't this done more than a year ago? Why didn't the Chamberlain Government organize labor in this way? Why weren't strikes outlawed months before, as was done on June 6? Why wasn't labor conscripted and the country organized at the end of 1938 and through 1939? This has all been done by Mr. Bevin, the new Minister for Labor under the Churchill Government. But Mr. Bevin was the great leader of the Trade Unions in England before the war. What was his and Mr. Greenwood's attitude at that time about this labor problem?

On October 6, 1938, alarmed by the great activity taking place in industry because of the armament program, Mr. Greenwood, on behalf of the Labour

Party, said, "There is the experience of the Great War to guide us, and we are not in a mood to tolerate any Derby scheme [reference to World War organization of labor] or any attempt to establish conscription by backstair methods." During the next few months, although Labour stressed its willingness to co-operate in the voluntary National Service scheme of the Government, it was firm against anything that appeared like industrial and military conscription.

The situation came to a head in March when Hitler invaded Prague. It now became evident to all that the hope of a permanent peace for Europe was doomed. The invasion of Prague meant the end of the Chamberlain policy of appeasement, and it meant, in addition, the desertion of the traditional policy of refusal to make commitments in Eastern Europe. The Government realized that something would have to be done to build back British prestige, to bring to the world a realization that from this time on appeasement was officially dead, and that England now was really determined to resist German attempts at expansion. For this reason it was decided to introduce military conscription, which up to now the Government had consistently promised it would never introduce while the country was at peace.

The opposition which met this scheme illustrates

clearly how entrenched was the Englishman's traditional love of freedom and how great was Labour's
fear of anything that appeared like conscription of
labor. Attlee, for the Labour Party, came out vigorously against it, because he believes that, "Far from
strengthening this country, it will weaken and di-
vide it, at a time when it should be strong and
united."

For the Liberal Party, Sir Archibald Sinclair opposed it because "A more formidable response can
be obtained from a democracy by leadership than by
compulsion; and because . . . the voluntary system
best accords with the history and the traditions of
the British people." In arguments against this,
Hoare-Belisha pointed out the great shortage of
trained men, especially for important and difficult
jobs in anti-aircraft defense. Unless some sort of
compulsory training was introduced, they could
never, in off hours, get the necessary practice in handling their guns.

Conscription was finally voted in over the opposition of the Labour Party, although this opposition
was considerably weakened by Léon Blum's (the
French Labor leader) statement attacking the "contradiction between the opposition of Labor to the
Cabinet [for not doing enough to oppose Hitler]
and its opposition to conscription."

The subject of conscription has been touched upon, not to make British Labour a scapegoat, but rather to illustrate that men quickly forget what they did and said only a short time ago. From the present they see facts in a different perspective than they did in the past, and they find it difficult to analyze conditions as they were then. For this reason, in seeking to explain what now seems inexplicable, they seize upon a man or a group to be the scapegoat.

Labour's attitude was, of course, the result of failing to realize the strength and power of the German military machine. And this feeling was not confined to Labour. The Government itself was not aware of the extent of the effort that was made. Great appropriations were made in July, and it was announced that the expenditures for that year would amount to £750,000,000, more than two-thirds of the average budget and one-seventh of the total National income.

In America a similar percentage of our National income would call for an expenditure of over $10,000,000,000. An editorial in the London *Times* in July stated with pride that the figure was not far short of what Germany was reported to be spending *three years ago*. It failed completely to see the irony of this statement and added: "Today not only are we much stronger than a year ago, but we are strong, judged by any standard." This attitude was to cost her dearly. Through this summer, figures were brought out to show that British plane production was now at 800 to 1000 a month, and progress was reported in all departments.

The summer of 1939 saw the dying gasp of appeasement in the Hudson-Wohlthat discussions about a gigantic loan to Germany from England. Hudson was Secretary to the Department for Overseas Trade, and Wohlthat was a right-hand economic expert of Goering's. Conversations were carried on between the two in which a plan was discussed by which Britain would lend Germany enough capital so that she could convert her armament industries back into peaceful production. This plan got nowhere as it was inadvertently disclosed, and public protests quickly killed it. But it is valuable as an indication that many British still felt the troubles of Europe were primarily economic, and were problems that could be ironed out without resorting to war.

The feeling of having done their utmost for peace, combined with a feeling of confidence in their new armed power, gave Britain an entirely different attitude in September 1939 from that of the previous year. The result was a feeling of grim determination among the Government and the people. Plans proceeded efficiently and with few hitches. The Balloon Barrage was complete, as were the anti-aircraft defenses, and the evacuation plans went through on schedule.

The result was that Britain felt secure in her defenses and believed that if they could get through the winter without a knockout blow, England would have so built up her defenses that she would easily be able to outlast Germany. Even when she saw Poland annihilated, the defeat was ascribed in England, as it was in America, to the lack of a sufficient air force. Military experts, in England and America, were confident that it would be an entirely different situation when the Nazis came up against the Maginot Line. For that reason England failed to make the sacrifices necessary to enable her to catch up to Germany. It was not until March that an editorial in *The Times* hailed the meeting in which the Trade Unions agreed to "dilution," and the introduction of women in skilled industry. The Government failed to make use of the 1,300,000 still unemployed, a contrast to the organization in Germany, which had suffered a labor shortage since 1935.

At the same time, England was also suffering from a serious shortage of skilled labor in many key industries manufacturing military necessities and goods for the vital export trade. Little was done to register the workers, or to make any great efforts to provide training for the thousands of unskilled workers who could, in a short time, have been shown the fundamentals of a new craft.

This feeling that all was going well was enhanced by Sir Kingsley-Wood's report in Commons in March. He reported that the output of planes had been doubled in the production of Spitfires and Hanker fighters, and that heavy bombers had been increased by fifty per cent. He stated that Allied plane production was now equal to Germany's. This was evidently too optimistic a statement, as, according to Washington estimates, Germany was turning out 2300 planes a month, 43 per cent more than Great Britain and France. Britain was turning out 1200 a month, and France, which early in 1939 had been turning out only 40 a month, was now producing 400. Against this combined figure of 1600 Germany's production was 2300. To balance that disparity to some extent, over 6000 bombers and 2000 ships of other types had been ordered in America.

Simon's budget, submitted in April, showed that the enormity of the effort needed was not yet fully realized. Although it was for a gigantic sum, over £2,000,000,000, England was spending only 52 per cent of Britain's national income, while Germany and France were spending over 60 per cent.

This situation, of course, was completely changed by the failure of the Norwegian expedition. This brought criticism of the Government to a head and a shift was effected in the Cabinet. This shift coincided with the invasion of Holland by Hitler. Churchill replaced Chamberlain; Sir Archibald Sinclair, Liberal leader, replaced Sir Samuel Hoare, who only a short time before had replaced Sir Kingsley-Wood as Air Minister. Eden came in as War Minister; Alexander, former first Lord of the Admiralty in the Labour Government of 1929–31, came into his old post; Herbert Morrison took the Ministry of Supply, Ernest Bevin took over the Ministry of Labour, and Lord Beaverbrook was appointed to the task of increasing the air production.

The fresh impetus that these men gave to the jobs, combined with a realization of the seriousness of the struggle that England was now facing, had a great effect on the country's effort. Powers were granted to Churchill equal with Hitler's; strikes and lockouts were forbidden; labor worked overtime on a seven-day week. And as a result, great strides were made in production. On June 6, Duff-Cooper announced Britain was almost on a parity with Germany in regard to aircraft production; and Bevin announced that some plants had increased production by more than 100 per cent.

With this new spirit alive in England my story ends. England was now awake; it had taken a great shock to bring home a realization of the enormity of the task it was facing. All the latent energy stored up in England during the last seven years is being expended in a vigorous drive for victory. Industry and labor, the rich and the poor, are contributing to England's fight for survival, with the knowledge that this is a supreme test of democracy's ability to survive in this changing world.

PART THREE

Conclusion

X

America's Lesson

IN THIS BOOK I have discussed some of the conditions responsible for Britain's position today. I commenced with the assumption that there was no short-cut to an understanding of this problem.

At times it may appear that I have tried unjustifiably to clear the leaders of responsibility. That is not my view. But I believe, as I have stated frequently, that leaders are responsible for their failures only in the governing sector and cannot be held responsible for the failure of a nation as a whole.

As long as England was a democracy, a democracy with a Parliamentary system, as long as the leaders could have been turned out of office at any time on any issue, Parliament, and hence those who elect the Parliament, must all bear their share of the responsibility.

This is not merely a pro-Baldwin or anti-Baldwin, a pro-Chamberlain or anti-Chamberlain discussion. I believe it is one of democracy's failings that it seeks to make scapegoats for its own weaknesses. A nation takes a long time to change its mind; but, although the change may be gradual, one slight shock may make it change with lightning speed from one position to another. It then frequently forgets the reasons for its previous point of view; it cannot understand how it could have believed as it formerly did. Seeking to explain this, it places the blame on the men who were then in office.

Herbert Morrison, the able British Labour leader, expressed this thought in simple and direct words when he was being criticized in 1939 for co-operating with the Government in their voluntary National Service:

At the beginning I got plenty of abuse from the irresponsibles because I said that Labour administrators must play their full part in A.R.P., which was denounced as a fraud and a plot of Ministers to create war psychology. For Labour local authorities to co-operate with state departments in this task was treachery. Anyway, no A.R.P. could possibly be effective.

And now? Well, my critics at that time are now among the noisiest, if not always the most effective, agitators for a vigorous A.R.P. policy. Before, *all* A.R.P. was a snare and a delusion. Today? Well, today we cannot have enough A.R.P. Yesterday, money spent on A.R.P. was waste. Today? Well, you can't spend too much.

It would be a better world (I feel confident that Lenin

would give a vigorous 'Hear, hear' to this) if some comrades would think and look ahead before they blether.

My reason for trying to ascertain in what measure each group was responsible was because I believed that to dismiss the matter purely as a question of poor leadership would mean that America would lose the benefit of the experience England has been going through.

In 1930 and 1931 we blamed all the evils that this country was then suffering, from the drought to the World Depression, on Herbert Hoover. If we had continued to hold those beliefs, we would never have learned anything from that experience. We would have dismissed it as being a question of leadership, and would have done nothing to prevent such an experience from happening again. It is, therefore, because I believe England's experience holds such a vital lesson for us, that I have sought to get away from the scapegoat idea.

For England has been a testing ground. It has been a case of a democratic form of government, with a capitalistic economy, trying to compete with the new totalitarian system, based on an economy of rigid state control. For a country whose government and economic structure is similar to England's and which may some day be similarly in competition with a dictatorship, there should be a valuable lesson.

It will be necessary first for us to ascertain how much of the responsibility for what has befallen England can be attributed to factors peculiarly England's and how much may be attributed to the more general weakness of democracy and capitalism.

Of the factors peculiarly English—that is, factors that we necessarily will not duplicate in this country—we may first set down England's leadership during this period. There is no doubt that she was unfortunate to have a man like Baldwin, with his lack of vision, in office at a particular period when vision above all else was needed. England needed a man who was able to look beyond the immediate situation and form some just estimate of changing conditions and eventualities in the future. Likewise with Chamberlain, a man who wished so intensely for peace, and had such sincere and strong hopes in the possibility of achieving it that he failed completely to estimate the dire need of his country to prepare for war.

In addition there was a great lack of young progressive and able leaders. Those who should have been taking over were members of the war generation, so large a portion of whom rested in Flanders fields. Men like Malcolm MacDonald and Anthony Eden were considered to be still too young.

Next comes the technical problems that England

faced, and which we do not share. Our industrial system is much more adaptable to mass production than was England's, which needed a complete transformation.

Then there is the English Parliamentary system, which is entirely different from ours. In England the opposition party is the Labour Party. And Labour naturally did not wish to lose its identity by joining wholeheartedly with the Government on an armaments program, especially when it believed that the Government was strongly sympathetic to much of the German system. This latter view was strengthened at Munich. The unfortunate part was that the Labour Party in Parliament represented skilled labor, the Trade Unions, upon which the success of any armaments program depends. This tie-up between the skilled labor necessary to the Government's program and the opposition of its Parliamentary representation to the Government, made the unification which the country so needed, difficult to attain. We, of course, do not have that same particular Parliamentary situation to face. Our "Opposition," the Republican Party, is not a class party, it represents no one particular economic group as did the English Labour Party.

In addition to these factors, there were others, such as the strong League sentiment and the Disarmament Conference, that affected armaments. Then there was the closeness to the Government of the English aristocracy which was opposed so strongly to war: some because they had strong "rightists" sympathies with Germany, some because they realized it would mean the end of their particular position, and some because they had a clear conception of what it would mean to England as a whole.

These, briefly, are some of the factors that contributed to England's tardiness in rearming, which we in America do not necessarily share. On the other hand, we can attribute our failure to rearm in part to factors that have no English counterpart, such as the strong feeling of isolation which exists in the Middle West, and the reaction of many people to the failure of European countries to pay their World War debts to the United States, which was one of determining to have no further share in European troubles. But I am interested in the broader aspects, and hence that we should not become involved in any foreign wars: what part of democracy and capitalism played in England's failure.

In regard to capitalism, we observe first that it was obedience to its principles that contributed so largely to England's failure. It has been estimated in authoritative circles that Hitler has spent anywhere from $50,000,000,000 to $100,000,000,000 in building up Germany's armaments. He ran Germany's debt to skyrocket heights and saved Germany from suffering violent inflation only by rigid state control.

How, therefore, could England have hoped to match his effort? When England's governmental revenue was less than $5,000,000,000 a year, she could not hope to do so over a very long period of time without going bankrupt. She, too, would have had to initiate rigid state control to prevent inflation and that would have been the end of capitalism and democracy. It may be argued that she could have sold her investments in other countries. But if she had done that, with the unfavorable balance of trade which she had had in the last few years, she could not have continued to pay for her imports. It would have meant ruin either way, and so naturally England was unwilling, *until she knew war was imminent,* to take the risk of making huge expenditures. America has gotten a taste of the same problem with her appropriations of around $13,000,000,000 this year. If she has to keep up this type of effort, or in fact anything remotely similar for seven or eight years, it will mean either a violent cut in relief expenditures, which will cause social unrest, or a great danger of inflation. And we are much richer than England. This then is a factor that must be considered in discussing Britain's effort, and in evaluating the ability of a capitalist economy to compete with a dictatorship.

How much did democracy's weakness contribute to England's present position? In the first place, democracy is essentially peace-loving; the people don't want to go to war. When they do go, it is with a very firm conviction, because they must believe deeply and strongly in their cause before they consent. This gives them an advantage over a totalitarian system, where the people may find themselves in a war in which they only half believe. Nevertheless, the hatred of war is, in this day of modern warfare, a great disadvantage. It takes years to prepare for modern mechanized warfare. It takes months of training for men to be able to handle the new machines. Democracy's spirit alone cannot make up this difference. This has been brutally proved by recent events. The result is that people, because of their hatred of war, will not permit armaments to be built. They are so determined to stay out that they cannot look ahead to the day when they will find occasion to fight. Woodrow Wilson was elected on a platform of "He kept us out of war," and yet, shortly after, America was at war with Germany. Nowadays, however, simply a sudden willingness to go to war will not prepare you for war. The plans have to be made years in advance, and it is extremely difficult to get support for this in a democracy.

This had an important effect on England's efforts. The people for a long time would not have tolerated any great armaments program. Even though Churchill vigorously pointed out the dangers, the people were much more ready to put their confidence in those who favored a strong peace policy. The result of this attitude is that a democracy will always be behind a dictatorship. In a dictatorship, a vigorous armaments program can be carried on, even though the people are deeply hostile to the idea of going to war. The rigidly controlled state press can then build up a war psychology at any time. In contrast, in a democracy the cry of "war-monger" will discourage any politician who advocates a vigorous arms policy. This leaves armaments with few supporters.

There is no lobby for armaments as there is for relief or for agriculture. No group backed by millions of votes can persuade the representatives of the people that *this* is what the people want. The business lobby will oppose armament, as it did in the Congress of American Industry Proclamation and that of the American Chamber of Commerce in 1938.

The lobbies of agriculture and relief will oppose it, as it would mean taking money from their cause for something in which they are not directly interested. This happened in our Congress in the first part of 1940.

And so armaments must stand purely on the ground of military necessity, and it is difficult for the average legislator to look far into the future; he is primarily concerned with the immediate problems.

I say, therefore, that democracy's weaknesses are great in competing with a totalitarian system. Democracy is the superior form of government, because it is based on a respect for man as a reasonable being. *For the long run,* then, democracy is superior. But for the short run, democracy has great weaknesses. When it competes with a system of government which cares nothing for permanency, a system built primarily for war, democracy, which is built primarily for peace, is at a disadvantage. And democracy must recognize its weaknesses; it must learn to safeguard its institutions if it hopes to survive.

In England we can see vividly where democracy failed. In the case of the A.R.P., for example, the Government failed to get volunteers until after Munich had driven home the seriousness of the situation. But Germany had 12,000,000 members by 1936. She needed no such shock to build up this vital defense measure. Should England have forced people to join? Yes, if the A.R.P. is considered the vital thing. No, if the democratic system is considered the important factor, as freedom of the individual is in essence democracy.

Again we witnessed the struggle between the National Government and the local government as to who should bear the burden of the cost of the A.R.P. Should the Government have forced the local authorities to provide their quotas? Freedom of local governments from centralized control is one of the cornerstones upon which we have erected our democracy.

Should the Trade Union have been forced to cooperate with the Government long before May of 1940? Should strikes have been outlawed, labor standards disregarded, men forced to go into trades and do work to which they were opposed? The smashing of the Trade Union is symbolic of Fascism. The right of labor to strike, the right to decent wages and decent hours have been what democracy has boasted is fundamental to its success.

Much of the cause of England's failure may be attributed to the leaders. The great advantage a democracy is presumed to have over a dictatorship is that ability and not brute force is the qualification for leadership. Therefore, if a democracy cannot produce able leaders, its chance for survival is slight.

I say, therefore, that many of the very factors intrinsic in democracy resulted in England's falling further and further behind. For democracy and capitalism are institutions which are geared for a world at peace. It is our problem to find a method of protecting them in a world at war.

What does this signify for our country? We must be prepared to recognize democracy's weaknesses and capitalism's weaknesses in competition with a totalitarian form of government. We must realize that one is a system geared for peace, the other for war. We must recognize that while one may have greater endurance, it is not immune to swift destruction by the other.

It means that in preparing for war today, which takes such a long time and is so expensive, a democracy may be struck such a knockout blow by a totalitarian form of government, which has prepared for war over a long period, that she will not be able to bring in the latent advantages that she possesses. It is only in the long war that the advantages of a greater spirit and determination among the people will be effective.

And we must realize that a democracy finds it difficult to keep up this sustained effort over a long period of time, for the interests of the individual are not directly concerned with armaments. He must make a great personal sacrifice to build them up, and it is hard to maintain this sacrifice year in and year out. Especially is it complicated by the fact that a democracy's free press gives the speeches of the totalitarian leaders, who state their case in such a "reasonable" manner that it is hard always to see them as a menace.

Taking all these factors into consideration, to prepare for modern warfare, where all the energies of a country must be subordinated to this task, a totalitarian state does have a great advantage. A democracy will, indeed, be two years behind a dictatorship.

Coupled with these internal disadvantages, are the more obvious advantages that a dictator has in foreign policy. He can bring the might of a unified nation into any issue, whether he is strongly supported by his followers or not. The invasion of the Rhineland by Hitler, against the advice of his generals, illustrates this clearly. Munich illustrates it even more strongly. Neither the people of Germany nor those of England wished to go to war, but the wishes of the German people were smothered under the unity of totalitarianism, while in England the desire of the people for peace had a great effect in the final settlement.

The representatives of a democracy cannot run

contrary to the basic wishes of the people in any game of bluff. When the decision must be whether it will be peace or war, the fundamental instinct of man against war binds the hands of democratic leaders. In a dictatorship, on the other hand, people are often powerless to impress their wishes on the dictator until it is too late. The democracies know this; they know that the weight of public opinion in the dictatorship, which would ordinarily be inclined on the side of peace, will not be of decisive importance; they can't count on it to slow up the dictator. On the other hand, the dictator is able to know exactly how much the democracy is bluffing, because of the free press, radio, and so forth, and so can plan his moves accordingly.

These great advantages of a dictatorship must be recognized if we are ever to hope for a survival of our system. To ignore them today when it is being menaced would be suicidal.

It is right and proper to support vigorously our way of living as being the greatest in the world, but it is not right and proper to be blind to its weaknesses. We all recognize the tremendous weakness of totalitarianism. A great advantage that our free press should give us is an opportunity to recognize our own weaknesses as well as our own strength. In so recognizing them, we may be able to guard against them.

Briefly, it means we should recognize the advantage that a dictatorship has in preparing for modern warfare. If Britain is defeated, and we are in competition with the dictatorships, both economically and in trying to build up armaments, we shall be at a definite disadvantage. We may be able to survive because of our natural geographic position and our great natural wealth. Our way of life has allowed us to develop ourselves tremendously under these advantages, but we shall have to be prepared to make long-sustained sacrifices if we are to preserve this way of life in the future. We shall have the realization to sustain us that over the long run we can outlast them; but while the menace is there, all groups must be prepared to sacrifice many of the particular group interests for the national interest. By voluntary effort, we must be prepared to equal the centralized efforts of the dictators.

We must always keep our armaments equal to our commitments. Munich should teach us that; we must realize that any bluff will be called. We cannot tell anyone to keep out of our hemisphere unless our armaments *and the people behind these armaments* are prepared to back up the command, even to the ultimate point of going to war. There must be no doubt in anyone's mind, the decision must be automatic: if we debate, if we hesitate, if we question, it will be too late.

And if the decision goes to the British, we must be prepared to take our part in setting up a world order that will prevent the rise of a militaristic dictatorship. We withdrew from Europe in 1920 and refused to do anything to preserve the democracy we had helped to save. We thought that it made no difference to us what happened in Europe. We are beginning to realize that it does. Even from a purely selfish standpoint, we realized it when we voted our first $5,000,000,000 for defense.

I say therefore that we cannot afford to let England's experience pass unnoticed. Now that the world is ablaze, America has awakened to the problems facing it. But in the past, we have repeatedly refused to appropriate money for defense. We can't escape the fact that democracy in America, like democracy in England, has been asleep at the switch. If we had not been surrounded by oceans three and five thousand miles wide, we ourselves might be caving in at some Munich of the Western World.

To say that democracy has been awakened by the events of the last few weeks is not enough. Any person will awaken when the house is burning down.

What we need is an armed guard that will wake up when the fire first starts or, better yet, one that will not permit a fire to start at all.

We should profit by the lesson of England and make our democracy work. We must make it work right now. Any system of government will work when everything is going well. It's the system that functions in the pinches that survives.

Appendix

---

*Speech by Neville Chamberlain in Commons
on Occasion of Viscount Swinton's Resignation*
May 25, 1938

Referring to the resignation of Viscount Swinton,
Mr. Chamberlain proceeded:

"When he took office, with no powers of compulsion but only those of persuasion, he was called
upon, at short notice, to carry out an enormous expansion of the organization of the Air Force. He was
called upon to equip it with new types of machines
which had not passed the stage of design, and at the
same time to make all the necessary preparations for
the recruitment and training of the increased personnel which was necessary to man the force. Not
only that. He had to take account of what might
happen if the last emergency arose and if we should
be involved in war. He had to take account of the
fact that the capacity of the country was quite insufficient to maintain our forces in the early period of a
war, and he consequently had to devise and put into
operation a system under which the war potential of

NATIONAL DEFENSE EXPENDITURES OF THE WORLD

Sources: The Foreign Policy Association; other authorities as to 1938 and 1939. Figures show millions of dollars

	1932	1933	1934	1935	1936	1937	1938	1939
North America	699.0	575.3	748.6	947.7	1,004.8	1,049.4	1,123.0	—
United States	667.8	540.3	710.0	911.7	964.9	992.1	1,065.7	1,162.6
Europe	2,458.0	2,690.8	3,519.4	7,053.7	11,185.4	12,806.9	14,211.4	—
Britain	426.1	455.5	480.6	595.6	846.9	1,263.1	1,693.3	1,817.1
France...............	509.2	678.8	582.7	623.8	834.4	909.2	731.5	1,800.2
Germany	253.5	299.5	381.5	2,600.0	3,600.0	4,000.0	4,400.0	4,500.1
Italy	270.6	241.2	263.7	778.1	916.1	573.4	526.0	873.4
U.S.S.R.	282.5	309.5	1,000.0	1,640.0	4,002.4	5,026.0	1,352.2	1,500.1
Far East (6 countries)	469.7	538.3	573.6	598.3	666.7	1,431.4	2,056.9	—
Japan	199.1	253.1	271.9	296.2	305.1	1,120.8	1,755.3	1,600.8
China	93.0	108.1	112.5	93.1	95.3	95.3	95.3	—
World total (60 countries) ...	3,783.7	3,962.8	5,031.4	8,776.0	12,976.0	15,468.7	17,581.3	20,000.1

GREAT BRITAIN'S WAR CHARGES EXPENDITURE *

War Debt Services and Armaments

(Amounts are in £'s millions)

	1913–14	1930–31	1931–32	1932–33	1933–34	1934–35	1935–36	1936–37	Estimates 1937–38	Estimates 1938–39	Estimates 1939–40
Army	28.4	40.0	38.5	36.0	37.5	39.6	44.9	49.3	90.7e	125.0e	165.0e
Navy	48.7	52.3	51.0	50.1	53.6	56.6	64.9	81.3	105.0	128.0e	149.5
Air Force	—	17.2	17.4	16.6	16.2	17.2	27.6	50.7	82.5	134.5	208.0
Civil Defence	—	—	—	—	—	—	—	—	—	18.0	56.5
Supplementary Estimates	—	—	—	—	—	—	—	—	—	—	20.0
Total Expenditures on Armaments .	77.1	109.5	106.9	102.7	107.3	113.4	137.4	181.3	278.2	405.5	599.0f
War Debt Services.	—	360.0	322.0a	308.5a	224.0b	224.0b	224.0b	224.0b	224.0b	230.0b	230.0b
War Pensions	—	51.7	49.4	46.8	45.2	43.1	42.4	41.4	40.5	43.1	42.1
Totals		521.2	478.3	458.0	376.5	380.5	403.8	446.7	542.7	678.6	871.1

Wholesale Price Index c   1913–100%   1938–98.9%
Cost of Living Index d   1914–100%   1938–156%

a The amounts allocated for the new Sinking Fund in each of these years were approximately £30,000,000 less than the figure for 1930–31.
b The heavy reduction on the 1932–33 figures is accounted for by the omission of any provision for the Sinking Fund, and by the decrease of some £50,000,000 in Debt Charges due to Conversion.   c Economist.   d Ministry of Labour.   e Includes Ordnance.
f Sir John Simon, the Chancellor of the Exchequer, in introducing his Budget on April 25th, 1939, pointed out that in a White Paper issued in February it was stated that defence expenditure was then estimated at £580,000,000 and said that this figure "is no longer correct or valid . . . We must now proceed on the assumption that something in the region of £630,000,000 will be required . . . It may well be more."
* Source: Peace Year Book, 1940.

the country could be increased to an extent which had not hitherto been dreamt of. To do that he necessarily had to enlist the services of firms who were entirely without previous experience of the work they were called upon to do.

"Those three years of which I speak during which the expansion of the Air Force has had to take place coincided with one of those forward leaps which periodically take place in applied science, and in this particular case the features of this advance took three forms. The development of the all-metal monoplane, the design of new engines of unprecedented efficiency, and the invention of the variable pitch air screw. The combination of those three new features in aircraft construction not only completely altered the design but it necessarily altered the strategy which had to be employed in the use of these newly developed machines.

"Lord Swinton's work during those three years has been largely one of building foundations, and we are now beginning to see the fruits of his labours. I have not the slightest doubt that upon the foundations which he has laid, my right hon. Friend the Secretary of State for Air will be able to build a firmly based structure of further additions and developments. But there are three indispensable pieces of preparatory work which have been done by Lord

Swinton, and for which we owe him gratitude. First of all he has consistently stimulated experimentation so that we might get the best types of machines that could be devised, and I think it is satisfactory that the orders that we have been placing recently are orders for machines which have the highest records for performance and for maintenance when they are actually in operation.

"The second task of my Noble Friend was to devise a scheme for the expansion and for the training of personnel. . . . In accordance with the plan of the Air Ministry, there are now 13 civil schools devoted to preliminary training, there are 11 training schools for Service flying, the capacity for the trade training of men and boys in the Air Service has been increased seven-fold, and Lord Swinton also created the Royal Air Force Volunteer Reserve, for which there are now 22 centres in operation. I am not sure whether hon. Members have already been told, but there are now over 1,000 volunteer pilots who have qualified to fly solo.

"Then may I say one word about the new war potential? That involved the building of new factories and very large extensions of those which were already engaged in aircraft construction. It also involved the creation of a shadow factory system, which, for the time being, is being fully employed, while we are building up the Force, but which it is intended later on to keep in reserve for an emergency only, placing with the shadow factories such orders as are necessary to maintain the craftsmanship and the experience of those who will run them. This shadow factory system is giving us an enormous increase of productive capacity in war and it covers not only the manufacture of aircraft and engines, but there are shadow factories also for the production of carburettors, bombs, and air screws. These factories are laid out on the very latest model of factory equipment, and they are, I am told, second to none in the world."

Speech by Viscount Swinton Regarding Difficulties Encountered by British in Building up Air Arm

May 12, 1938

Viscount Swinton said: "The House is well aware that there were serious initial delays in the output of aircraft. The scale on which orders were placed—and the industry had never had large-scale orders before; it could not have them—was such that much time was necessarily spent in constructing new shops and in arranging for the supply of jigs and tools necessary for large-scale production. Expansion also coincided with the development of an entirely new

technique in manufacture in which British industry
had had little, if any, opportunity of taking part—the
development of large all-metal skin-dressed types of
aircraft. Also, as the House is well aware, there was a
great shortage of skilled labour, a shortage all the
more serious because the great demands of the aircraft industry coincided with a great expansion of
ordinary civil industry, both alike making demands
on the same kind of labour; and the policy was being
pursued at that time, and reasonably pursued, of interfering as little as possible with the ordinary trade
of the country which was then entering upon its
expansion.

"But the Air Ministry, in making their plans,
looked forward, and were indeed bound to look forward, to the probable need of a larger programme
and of acceleration, whether the larger programme
or the existing programme held the field. They
therefore planned on a large scale. Factory extensions, new factories, shadow factories were created of
a size which would not only cope with orders which
were then given, but which, with little further ex-
tension, would be on a scale and of a size to cope
with a much larger output. If that had not been
done it would not be possible today to place orders
and get going immediately a much larger programme
than that on which we have been at work. I empha-

sise that because it was that preparation, that laying-out of factories on an extensive scale, which alone makes possible much that we are putting in hand at the present time.

"And just as the Air Ministry planned the factories on a larger scale than was required for the initial programme, so they also planned to have the training establishments within the Air Force larger. . . . The Air Ministry also planned the orders which would be necessary if the programme were extended. The result of that preparatory work—preparatory work which it obviously was the duty of the Air Ministry to undertake—was that, when a decision was taken that the expansion should go further, it was possible to take immediately effective action.

"The objective of the Government in the decision that has been taken is twofold. It is both to speed up and to enlarge the programme . . . In aircraft the acceleration of the new expansion orders which have been given should mean an increase in output in this financial year of well over 50 per cent., and doubling this year's output during the next financial year. That is a very great increase of production, which is already substantial, and it is the considered opinion of those in the industry that that production can and will be obtained, on one condition, and that is that the necessary labour is available.

"As a result of the preparation which went before, and that practical method of giving effect to the preparation, firms which can produce the aircraft required by the programme—and it is the right kind of aircraft which it is necessary to have and not just any aircraft which you can order anywhere, as your Lordships will fully appreciate—have received additional orders which will fill them to the maximum of their capacity in plant and labour for the next two years. The great production must come from the factories of a size and capacity to work on that scale. Large-scale orders running into hundreds in a factory of a single type must be placed with factories which have both the experience and the works capacity to execute them. Smaller works can perform and are performing most valuable services in sub-contracting, and I know it is the policy of the firms to sub-contract wherever they possibly can, and can get good results, in order to increase the output of the works.

"We are also using some of these smaller firms to do repair work and that is proving successful. It obviates the expense and the delay of creating additional repair facilities within the Air Force itself; it keeps the main firms in a steady flow of production; and it enables the smaller firms to undertake repair work on damaged machines—one particular type going to one particular factory—work which they are doing very satisfactorily. It is a system which we should wish to expand. I have shown, I think, that there is no case of placing orders in driblets. The policy has always been to give the largest orders which are authorised by the programme."

Speech by Neville Chamberlain Regarding Proposal for Ministry of Supply

May 25, 1938

Dealing with the proposal to form a Ministry of Supply, Mr. Chamberlain continued: "Whichever form of ministry of supply we adopt it must inevitably mean a certain dislocation of the present machine, and that must be followed, therefore, by a check and a setback in the programme which is being developed by the existing organisation. It seems to me that that difficulty is only to be overridden if there are some superior interests to be served. Either the new ministry of supply will be so superior to the present system that it will very quickly overtake the arrears, and thereafter give us greatly increased output, or else it follows that the present system is deficient in co-ordination, and that the new scheme would put an end to that deficiency and consequently promote efficiency and progress, which are now being hampered by overlapping.

"There is ample machinery existing today and working daily for preventing overlapping and for allocating priority in all the things that matter. I wonder sometimes whether hon. Members realise how far the system of co-ordination has been carried today in commodities which we require for warlike purposes. The House has been told on other occasions of a body which is known as the Principal Supply Officers' Committee—a sub-committee of the Committee of Imperial Defence. That is the body which is responsible for this work. It contains representatives of all the Departments that are concerned in war supplies—the three Service Departments, the Treasury, the Board of Trade, the Ministry of Labour, the Home Office, and also the Dominions and India. It deals with all the commodities that are required in war—ships, guns, aeroplanes, tanks, explosives and propellants, motor vehicles, clothing, raw materials, machine tools and so forth. I could enlarge the list almost indefinitely. It is in continuous session.

"In the case of every one of these commodities—and I have given only some—it assesses what would be the probable demand for that commodity in wartime, based, of course, on certain hypotheses as to the conditions of the war. It has inspected hundreds of factories all through the country. It has now allocated the capacity for each of these commodities, and where the capacity does not fully exist it has taken, or is taking, steps to supply the deficiency. It handles all questions of priority as between one Department and another, and that covers not only materials but labour. It has the closest relations with industry because it has on its representatives of industry, leading men who are in close touch with it and who act, in fact, as chairmen of some of its sub-committees. This is an organisation which was founded as long ago as 1924. It has been gradually building up this system. There was nothing like it before 1914, before the Great War, and I am bound to say that I find great difficulty in seeing how it will be possible to improve upon it today for the particular purposes for which it has been constituted.

"My own view—and I, at any rate, have not looked at this matter from any departmental point of view; I am not concerned with the prestige of one Department against another—is that, although in actual war a ministry of supply would be essential—and, indeed, we have all the plans ready for such a ministry which could be put into operation at once in such circumstances—I do not believe that a ministry of supply in peacetime will be effective, as the Ministry of Munitions was effective in the Great War, unless you give that ministry of supply the same powers as the Ministry of Munitions had.

"I submit to hon. Members that you can do a great deal today by persuasion, by voluntary effort, and by co-operation with labour and with employers; but if you want to produce the sort of effect you had in the Great War, when the Government had absolute control over the whole of industry throughout the country, you must give this ministry the same sort of powers.

"What I am saying is that I do not think it is any use setting up a ministry of supply with the same limited powers that we have already. If you want to go further than that you must have these further powers over industry and over labour, and I doubt very much whether we should be justified in asking for such powers, or whether, if we did ask for them, Parliament would give us them in time of peace. The analogy of wartime is really misleading. We are not at war.

"I have said repeatedly in many Debates on this subject that our programme is flexible; it is a programme which is capable of expansion, or even of reduction; and it is a programme, therefore, which must vary from time to time in accordance with the international situation. I do not mind saying—and I pick out here something which I think I heard just now—that to me the important thing is not the programme but its execution. What the Government have set themselves to do is to get the maximum execution possible, at least in the next two years. In these days, when foreign conditions are continually changing, it is difficult to look forward with any confidence to what the conditions may be over a longer period than two years, but our view is that it is our duty to obtain the maximum production of aircraft, and all the necessary accessories and equipment, that this country can give us in the course of the next two years. That is really the programme we have set before ourselves for the present."

Bibliography

BOOKS

ANGELL, NORMAN—*The Defence of the Empire*, Hamish Hamilton, London, 1937

BALDWIN, STANLEY—*Service of Our Lives*, Hodder & Stoughton, London, 1937

BECHHOFER, ROBERT—*Stanley Baldwin, Man or Miracle?* Greenberg, London, 1937

BRIFFAULT, ROBERT—*The Decline and Fall of the British Empire*, Simon and Schuster, New York, 1938

British War Blue Book (Misc. # 9), Farrar & Rinehart, Inc., New York, 1939

BROMFIELD, LOUIS—*England: A Dying Oligarchy*, Harper & Bros., New York, 1939

BROWN HODGES, ROUCEK—*Contemporary World Politics*, John Wiley & Sons, London, 1939

CAMBON, JULES—*Foreign Policy of Powers*, Harper & Bros., New York, 1935

CHAMBERLAIN, NEVILLE—*The Struggle for Peace*, Hutchinson & Co., London, 1939

CHURCHILL, WINSTON S.—*Step By Step* (1936–1939), G. P. Putnam's Sons, New York, 1939

CHURCHILL, WINSTON S.—*While England Slept*, G. P. Putnam's Sons, New York, 1938

CRIPPS, SIR STAFFORD, and other labor leaders—*Problems of Socialist Government*, Victor Gollancz

DUFF-COOPER, ALFRED—*The Second World War (First Phase)*, Charles Scribner's Sons, New York, 1939

EDEN, ANTHONY—*Foreign Affairs,* Faber and Faber, London, 1939

ENGELY, GIOVANNI—*Politics of Naval Disarmament,* Williams and Norgate, London, 1932

GATHORNE-HARDY, G. M.—*A Short History of International Affairs, 1920–1938,* Oxford, 1938

GUNTHER, JOHN—*Inside Europe,* Harper & Bros., New York, 1938

HEARNSHAW, F. J. C.—*Prelude to 1937,* John Murray, London

HOLLIS, CHRISTOPHER—*We Aren't So Dumb*—Longmans, Green & Co., London, 1937

HOLLIS, CHRISTOPHER—*Foreigners Aren't Fools,* Fred A. Stokes, New York, 1937

KENWORTHY, J. M.—*Peace or War?* Boni & Liveright, New York, 1927

KING-HALL, STEPHEN—*Our Own Times, Volume I,* Ivor Nicholson & Watson, London, 1934

KING-HALL, STEPHEN—*Our Own Times, Volume II,* Ivor Nicholson & Watson, London, 1935

KIRKPATRICK, HELEN P.—*Under the British Umbrella,* Charles Scribner's Sons, New York, 1939

LAJOS, DR. IVAN—*Germany's War Chances,* Victor Gollancz, London, 1939

League of Nations, Armaments Year Books, 1925–1933

LIDDELL-HART—*Defence of Britain*

LIVINGSTONE, DAME ADELAIDE—*The Peace Ballot,* Victor Gollancz, London, 1935

MACKINTOSH, JOHN—*The Paths That Led to War,* Black & Sons, London, 1940

MADARIAGA, SALVADOR DE—*Disarmament,* Coward, McCann, New York, 1929

MOWRER, EDGAR ANSEL—*Germany Puts the Clock Back*

(July 20, 1932, to September 3, 1939), William Morrow,
New York, 1939

NICHOLS, BEVERLY—*Cry Havoc!* Jonathan Cape, London,
1933

Political Handbook of the World, 1928–1939, Council of
Foreign Relations, New York

RAUSCHNING, HERMANN—*The Revolution of Nihilism,* Longmans, Green & Co., London, 1939

SALTER, SIR ARTHUR—*Security, Can We Retrieve It?* Reynal
and Hitchcock, New York, 1939

SCHUMAN, FREDERICK L.—*Europe on the Eve,* Alfred A.
Knopf, New York, 1939

SETON-WATSON, R. W.—*Britain and the Dictators,* Macmil-
lan, New York, 1938

SPENDER, JOHN ALFRED—*Great Britain, Empire and Com-
monwealth,* Cassell & Co., London, 1936

TOYNBEE, A. J.—*Future of the League of Nations,* Oxford,
1936

TOYNBEE, A. J.—*Surveys of International Affairs, 1923–1938,*
Oxford

VIGILANTES—*Inquest on Peace,* Victor Gollancz, London,
1935

VIGILANTES—*The Road to War,* Victor Gollancz, London,
1937

VON PUCKLER—*How Strong Is Britain?* George Routledge,
London, 1939

WHEELER-BENNETT, JOHN W.—*Disarmament and Security,*
Allen & Unwin, London, 1932

WHEELER-BENNETT, JOHN W.—*Documents on International
Affairs, 1931–38*

WHEELER-BENNETT, JOHN W.—*The Pipe Dream of Peace,*
William Morrow, New York, 1935

WITTMER, FELIX—*Floodlight on Europe,* Charles Scribner's
Sons, New York, 1937

International Conciliation Documents, 1935, Carnegie Endowment for International Peace, New York

International Conciliation Documents, 1938, Carnegie Endowment for International Peace, New York

PAMPHLETS AND MAGAZINES

Articles from The Saturday Review

    HALSBURY, LORD—*England in the Air,* January 1, 1929, August 26, 1933

    STEWART, O.—*Air and the Future,* April 15, 1933

    BROAD, H. S.—*Britain Must Build More Planes,* January 27, 1934

    BEAUMONT, C.—*Gambling With Our National Existence,* January 16, 1931

    GRANT, P.—*Sea Power and Air Power,* December 30, 1933

    WALDRON, E. A.—*Economy at the Cost of Human Life?* December 16, 1931

Articles from The Labour Monthly

    HUTT, A.—*Disarmament and the Coming War,* May 13, 1931

    DUTT, R. P.—*The Arms Plan,* April, 1937

    PRITT, D. N.—*The Arms Stampede,* April, 1937

    SHINWELL, E.—*Rearmament and the Labour Party,* May, 1937

    CAMPBELL, J. R.—*Next Steps for a United Front,* April, 1937

The English Review, February, 1933, *Grave Deficiencies of the Army* by Liddell-Hart

The Quarterly Review, January, 1933, *Armaments and British Prestige* by I. Phayre

The Public Opinion Quarterly, January, 1937, *British Public Opinion and Foreign Policy* by Harold Nicolson

The Queen's Quarterly, May, 1938, *Chamberlain's Policy and Canada* by A. E. Prince

Falconer Lectures, April 22, 1939

The Challenge of Disarmaments, Nos. I, II, III, IV

Documents on International Affairs by Wheeler-Bennett, 1932

The Fortnightly Review, October, 1938, *The Great Unprepared* by L. E. O. Charlton

The Contemporary Review, January, 1939, *The European Crisis and Britain's Military Situation* by Liddell-Hart

The Spectator, April 17, 1936, *Germany's Armed Strength*

The Political Quarterly, January-March, 1937, *Arms and Peace* by Leonard Woolf

The Nineteenth Century, March, 1939, *Bombing From the Air* by Lord Londonderry

The New Statesman and Nation, February 15, 1936, *Policy and Armaments* by Harold Nicolson

British Foreign Policy Since the War, by G. P. Gooch, 1936

Peace Year Books—1925–1939

Trade Unions Congress Report—1933–1939

The Economist—1933—February 18, 25; March 25; September 23

1934—February 10; March 24; September 1; November 3, 24; December 1

1935—February 16; March 16, 23; April 13; May 25; August 10, 16, 17; September 28; October 10, 12; November 23

1936—February 8; March 7; May 30; July 25; August 1

1937—June 4, 19; November 13, 27; December 11

1938—April 2, 9, 16, 23, 30; May 7, 14, 21; June 4

NEWSPAPERS

New York Times 1936–1938
London Times 1931–1939
Manchester Guardian